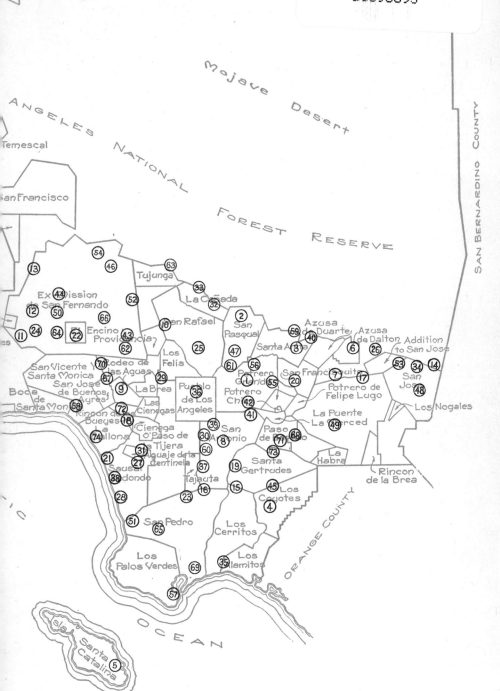

KERN COUNTY

mos Y Agua Caliente
iebre

Mojave Desert

ANGELES NATIONAL

Temescal

San Francisco

FOREST RESERVE

SAN BERNARDINO COUNTY

54
46
63
Tujunga
13
33
La Cañada
Ex Mission 44 52 32
de San Fernando
12 50 San Rafael 2
66 San
64 22 Encino 43 10 Pasqual 47 Azusa
11 24 Providencia 62 25 Santa Anita 59 40 de Duarte Azusa
Los 56 6 26 de Dalton Addition
San Vicente 70 Rodeo de Felis 61 Potrero 7 17 53 34 14 to San Jose
Santa Monica 87 las Aguas 29 1 Grande San Francisquito 48 San Jose
San Jose 9 La Brea 36 55 20 Potrero de Los Nogales
Boca de Buenos 58 Pueblo Potrero Felipe Lugo
de Ayres de Los Chico 42
Santa Mon Rincon de 18 Angeles 41 La Puente
Bueyes 72 Las La Merced 49
74 Cienega 39 San 71 Paso
21 Ballona 31 O'Paso de 30 8 Antonio 73 de La Habra
Sausal 27 Tijera 60 Santa
Redondo 33 Aguaje de la 37 19 Gertrudes Rincon
Centinela 45 Los de la Brea
28 Tajauta 16 15 Coyotes
23 4 ORANGE COUNTY
51 San Pedro
65 Los
Cerritos
Los 69 35 Los
Palos Verdes Alamitos
57

OCEAN

Santa
Catalina 5

Ranchos Become Cities

☆ Ranchos Become Cities *is one of the* Adohr *series of books interesting to those who live and work in Southern California*

Ranchos Become Cities

by W. W. Robinson

With Illustrations

by IRENE ROBINSON

SAN PASQUAL PRESS
PASADENA, CALIFORNIA
1939

ACKNOWLEDGMENT

A series of booklets—calendars of events—by W. W. Robinson, published by Title Guarantee and Trust Company, Los Angeles, contained the foundation material of Ranchos Become Cities. *Acknowledgment is made of the generous courtesy of the Title Guarantee and Trust Company in permitting the publication, in revised form, of the substance of these booklets.*

Foreword

History today is greatly concerned with the social and economic institutions under which a people live. The roots of such institutions usually go very deep. In this volume Mr. W. W. Robinson treats of the early California land holding system—the most important legacy the state inherited from the Spanish-Mexican regime.

The very title of the book—*Ranchos Become Cities* —is indicative both of the historical significance and the romantic nature of the subject. From the three original grants of some hundreds of thousands of acres rather casually made by Governor Pedro Fages, in 1784, to Juan José Dominguez, José Manuel Nieto, and José Maria Verdugo, down through the secularization of the mission lands in 1833; the annexation of California by the United States; the decisions of the Federal Land Commission created by the Act of 1851; the long years of litigation in the courts; the ruin and bankruptcy resulting from exorbitant legal fees, compound interest ranging from three to ten per cent a month, extravagance and drought; the gradual break-up of the unfenced ranges (measured not in acres but in square leagues!); the creation of great cities; the rise of the southern California of today—thus runs the thread of the story—the tale the author tells as he traces the eventful development of some twenty of the great *ranchos* of

Los Angeles county from their origin as Spanish or Mexican grants into centers of a huge, rushing, complicated, metropolitan population.

Long experience in the field of land titles in California has signally qualified Mr. Robinson to write this book. All those who have any interest in the amazing social and economic evolution of Los Angeles county, or in its pastoral beginning, will be grateful to him for it.

ROBERT G. CLELAND

Occidental College
July 10, 1939

Contents

During the Pastoral Age

CALIFORNIA'S RANCHOS

THREE SPANISH SOLDIERS—California's three musketeers they might be called—became California's first ranchers. It happened in the fall of 1784.

The ranchos chosen were all in what is now Los Angeles County.

Juan José Dominguez, one of the "leather-jackets" who marched north to San Diego with Captain Rivera in 1769, showed the way to ranch ownership. From his hardboiled commander, Pedro Fages, governor of Alta California, he got the permit he asked for, and presently was driving a herd of horses and cattle from

9

San Diego to the site of what became California's first rancho—the San Pedro.

When Corporal José Maria Verdugo, on "detached service" at Mission San Gabriel, heard what Dominguez was doing, he asked a similar favor. The governor obliged him. And so was founded the Rancho San Rafael—within whose boundaries are Glendale and part of Burbank.

Manuel Nieto, the third musketeer, received a concession, too. He was allowed to put his cattle on the vast area that stretched from the Santa Ana to the San Gabriel Rivers and from the San Diego-San Gabriel Road to the sea. Many cities were to arise on Nieto's land, the largest of them Long Beach. Nieto built a hut southwest of the present Whittier. Other white men and their families joined him and before the year 1800 "Los Nietos" was patterned with fields where Indian servants worked. Manuel and his friends—Los Angeles County's first colony—owned thousands of cattle and horses.

So began the rancho movement—and the pastoral age—in California. By the year 1846, when the American military conquest started, ranchos extended from the San Diego County area in the south to the Shasta County area in the north. They took in most of the good valley and grazing land in the southern part of the state and much of that in the northern part.

The three first ranchers, it should be noted, received no grants from the King of Spain—in whom the title to the land had vested upon Spanish occupation in 1769. Instead, they got cattle-grazing permits, little more.

Talk of "Spanish grants" is largely misinformed. It comes chiefly from descendants of first settlers and from novelists, who like to think of a far distant king taking kindly thought of Californians and signing be-ribboned documents that gave whole valleys to favored and aristocratic men. These royal documents are elusive; they have a habit of never coming to light.

Governor Fages asked for official approval of the right to allot tracts of land, outside of pueblos, for cattle and sheep raising. It was given him in 1786, in a legal opinion from Galindo Navarro, written at Chihuahua, Mexico, on October 27, 1785, and transmitted by the Comandante General. Fages was told, however, that settlers must avoid injury to missions, pueblos and Indian villages, and that pasture lands in the allotted tracts were to remain "for the common advantage."

Such allotments of land were what many other rancheros—usually soldiers or ex-soldiers—got during the Spanish period that ended in 1822. Formal grants, likewise from governors, came in the Mexican period, especially after the year 1828 when land laws were clarified. Many of these were in confirmation of early Spanish concessions. Permits, allotments, grants—they were gifts of the government. Claims to land were passed upon by the United States Land Commission, created in 1851, successful claimants receiving—ultimately—patents from the United States.

During the pastoral age in California cattle raising was the chief use to which ranch land was put. The men of the ranchos occupied themselves with their cattle interests, the women with the household and with the education of the children. Indians acted as servants. Rigid simplicity marked the first years. The houses were huts, made of adobe bricks, with one, two or three rooms. From ship captains the ranch owners got such luxuries as tables and chairs, made in New England, and such fineries as silks and shawls, made in China. Rodeos, balls and church festivals gave flavor to living. Only in the later years and in the Fifties, however, did the rancheros live in the lavish manner pictured in stories and murals. A few brief years of prosperity to ranch owners followed the American influx to the gold fields, with increased demand for cattle products—then came the drought of the Sixties and with it bankruptcy, foreclosure, ranch partition, and the death of the pastoral age.

The story of the first ranch owners in California and of those who followed is not contained, in detail, in Bancroft, Hittell, and formal histories. It is to be found in sources almost entirely overlooked: the archives and *expedientes* (land grant files) of the Mexican period; in the proceedings of the United States Land Commission and of the United States courts; and, in lesser extent, in the court actions and documents that make up the public records of early American years. In this source material, people long dead come to life and testify to their way of daily living. Here are the letters dictated by men who could not write, concerned with the life-and-death matters of their cattle business, or, perhaps, with the ordering of manteca or aguardiente. Here are the disputes, amusing to present readers, between neighbors who died before President James K. Polk proclaimed, in 1846, that "a state of war exists" between the Republic of Mexico and the United States. Here spring into being men and women who lived generously and died piously in pastoral California.

These sources have been drawn upon—almost for the first time—in outlining the stories of *Ranchos Become Cities*. Less than twenty ranchos are included in this volume, and they are all in Los Angeles County, California's original "cow county." It would take many volumes to hold the stories of the five hundred and more ranchos that once flourished along the rivers and upon the good pasture lands of Spanish and Mexican California. Ranchos have become cities and the transformation is California's story.

Los Angeles Harbor as it appeared in 1769

SAN PEDRO – WILMINGTON

and the story of the
RANCHO SAN PEDRO
and the
RANCHO LOS PALOS VERDES

IN THE YEAR 1769, a ship captain sailing up the coast of California toward what is now San Pedro would have looked upon a long shore line, edged in white surf; sand dunes protecting a slough behind; and then the steep yellow bluffs and treeless hills rising back of San

14

Pedro Bay. Close by he would have noticed a small, conical peak rising out of the waters. He might also have seen canoes carrying brown Indians between the mainland and Santa Catalina, for the village of Suanga, composed of shell-fish eaters, was on the heights just back of the Inner Bay.

1769 Indian Canoes

It was in this year that the occupation of California by the Spanish began, under Gaspar de Portolá, governor of the Californias.

The ship captain's view was the same that Cabrillo had had in 1542 when he turned into what he called the "Bay of Smokes"—San Pedro, now Los Angeles Harbor—except that Cabrillo saw the brush fires and smoke of an Indian rabbit drive and named the place accordingly. A similar scene met the eyes of the navigator Viscaino, whose visit to this bay sixty years after Cabrillo's resulted in the name of "San Pedro"—derived from Saint Peter, bishop of Alexandria, the harbor having been entered on St. Peter's day.

It was a soldier of the Portolá occupation who founded Rancho San Pedro, within whose original area lie San Pedro and Wilmington.

The soldier was Juan José Dominguez, bearer of a name that is today one of southern California's best known.

When Dominguez was ready to retire he asked a favor of his commander, Governor Fages. Dominguez had cattle and horses and a place all picked out which had water, pasture-land and easy access to the three-year-old Pueblo of Los Angeles on the one side and to the Bay of San Pedro on the other. He wanted to settle on this place located on the San Gabriel River near the coast, the San Gabriel then following the channel of the Los Angeles River where it empties into the sea.

Unfortunately the correspondence between Dominguez and Fages was burned long ago, along with all direct records of the San Pedro Rancho prior to the year 1805. Other sources, however, including those dealing with the San Rafael Rancho, disclose that Fages gave Dominguez the permit he asked for and that sometime in 1784 a sixty-five-year-old ex-soldier left the "Royal Presidio of San Diego," driving a herd of horses and two hundred head of cattle to the selected site of what became California's first rancho. Dominguez' permit, in fact, was used as a precedent by another Spanish soldier, Verdugo, who later in the same year asked to be allowed to pasture cattle upon San Rafael.

1784
Dominguez
Comes

Dominguez, taking over his new possessions, built a home on the slope of a hill, several huts and corrals. The old leather-jacket was a bachelor and had only to provide for himself, his major-domo and his servants.

For twenty years he was destined to live on the Rancho San Pedro, whose boundaries on the west and south he considered to be the sea, thus including all of what later was segregated into the Rancho Los Palos Verdes. During that time his cattle increased in number, grazing upon the rolling land that stretched to the mud flats that became Wilmington and upon the hills rising back of San Pedro Bay. From his ranch he

could look toward a blue ocean and watch Spanish
ships, foreign smugglers and spouting whales.

This early period was recalled many years later by
a friend, Bacilio Valdez, when questions such as the
following were put to him on the witness stand in the
United States Land Commission hearings:

"Were you acquainted with Juan José Dominguez; if so, when and where did you first
make his acquaintance?

"*I knew him here on his Rancho of San
Pedro in the year 1799 . . . he had a house there
and a great number of horses and cattle. I went
there frequently to get cheese and meat.*"

"What sort of a house was there on the
Rancho San Pedro when you first knew it?"

"*The walls of the house were of adobe with
a wooded top covered with pitch. It might have
had one or two rooms and might have been ten
or twelve varas square; I don't recollect exactly
. . . the house was some distance from the road
. . . there is a slope just as you get into the hills.
There were corrals and huts.*"

"How long did Juan José Dominguez con-
tinue to live on the Rancho San Pedro after
1799?

"*He lived there five years and afterwards became blind and his nephew (Cristobal Dominguez) took care of him for three or four years*

in the Mission of San Juan Capistrano, where his nephew had command of the troops."

When Juan José Dominguez left his home to spend his last days at the Mission, he left behind him, in the care of his major-domo, 3000 mares, 1000 fillies, 1000 colts, 700 cows, 200 heifers and 260 bulls.

*1805
American
Ship*

Blind old Dominguez had already left for San Juan Capistrano when the American vessel, the *Lelia Byrd*, Captain William Shaler in command, arrived in 1805.

It anchored in the little harbor of Avalon, Santa Catalina Island, where its officers and crew could safely defy the Spanish law forbidding commerce between Californians and foreign ships and could send small boats carrying silks, shawls and shoes to San Pedro in exchange for hides.

This was the first American ship to appear off San Pedro.

*1809
Death at
Ninety*

Dominguez, dying at ninety, left as his only heir his nephew, Cristobal Dominguez.

Manuel Gutierrez, the executor of the old man's will, delivered possession of Rancho San Pedro to Cristobal, a soldier like his uncle.

Immediately after the success of the revolution of 1821, a young soldier named Sepulveda decided he wanted a ranch. He was José Dolores Sepulveda, whose immediate ancestors had come from Sinaloa, Mexico, in 1781, Francisco Xavier Sepulveda having been one of the soldiers who accompanied the first settlers to Los Angeles.

José Dolores, along with Antonio Machado, got the permission of Manuel Gutierrez to keep horses and cattle upon a portion of the Rancho San Pedro. Gutierrez held a life estate in the ranch given him years before by Juan José Dominguez.

Sepulveda moved his cattle into the new pasturage and by December of 1822 the first dispute of many disputes between the Sepulveda and Dominguez families was under way. Cristobal Dominguez was petitioning the Governor to make Sepulveda withdraw his 800 head of cattle from his rancho. "There ought to be but two branding irons," he said, meaning one for himself and one for Gutierrez.

1822
Sepulveda's
Cattle

The disputes did not end until the "Rancho Los Palos Verdes" was carved out of what Dominguez had thought to be his domain, and was granted, on the basis of long years of possession, to the Sepulveda family.

The name "Palos Verdes," meaning green trees, had its origin in the "Cañada de Palos Verdes," a canyon favored by early settlers and shown on old maps. Green with grass and willow trees, it lay between the present Sepulveda and Lomita Boulevards, east of Vermont and west of Figueroa. Water, collecting in the bottom, flowed on to Machado Lake, now Bixby Slough.

Today the Cañada de Palos Verdes is ringed with snorting oil derricks. In it are two or three dead willows to recall the small valley whose green beauty suggested the name of the great ranch on which the harbor city of San Pedro would arise.

One February day in 1824, while Sepulveda was

riding back from Monterey, where he had gone to discuss his claims to Rancho Los Palos Verdes with the Governor, he was unfortunate enough to stop in at the Misión de la Purisima Concepción. The neophytes on that day were in revolt and Indian arrows killed José Dolores Sepulveda.

This tragedy left five little Sepulvedas at San Pedro without a father. There were four boys—the oldest of whom was ten—Juan, Ygnacio, Diego, José and one girl, Maria Teresa, a baby of a few months,

A yellow-brown document in the Los Angeles archives inventories the articles that their guardian Enrique Sepulveda turned over to the children, from their father's possessions. Among them were:

Two coats of first class broadcloth with 35 silver buttons.

A pair of pants of first class cloth, without border and with gold buttons.

A case for barber's razors with two serviceable razors.

A decorated saber of silver, edge chipped, harness destroyed, decorated sheath, with three pieces broken.

A good shot gun, with wooden rod.

A pair of silver buckles for good spurs.

A trunk with lock and key.

No doubt these gifts were more prized than the ranch itself.

In 1827, the old records state, Governor Figueroa made the Sepulvedas a provisional concession of Rancho

Los Palos Verdes—the "place situated towards the Embarcadero."

Many years later, when the boy Juan had become a man of 61 and was explaining his claims before the Board of Land Commissioners, he said of this period:

"In the year 1824, the guardian of us petitioned Governor Echeandia for a provisional grant of the Rancho Palos Verdes to maintain our stock on. In that year our property was divided between us and our mother, she having married Antonio Machado. We were then living on the Rancho of Manuel Gutierrez, which is now that of Manuel Dominguez. In that year, and as aforesaid, our guardian made a petition for a grant, provisionally, of the Rancho Los Palos Verdes and Cerro San Pedro, and we went to that place with our stock, and from that date until the present time we have been living there."

When Cristobal Dominguez died in 1825 his twenty-two-year-old son, Manuel, took over the management of the ranch, and when he bought out his brother Nasario ten years later became its owner.

1825
Manuel
Dominguez

Manuel built an adobe home on the ranch for himself and his steadily increasing family. It stands today on a hillside near Dominguez junction, though it has been enlarged and remodeled, and is used as a seminary to train priests for the Claretian Order.

Manuel managed the ranch well and became one of the great cattle owners of southern California. At his ranch house he dealt out hospitality with lavish

hands. He was a member of the Los Angeles Ayuntamiento or Council, was first alcalde and judge, terri-
torial representative and captain of a military company;
and when he died in 1882 he left the ranch intact except for the Wilmington and other smaller portions
he had sold and deeded.

It was during this period and for many years after
that San Pedro was the largest hide-shipping port
on the coast, for trade restrictions had been removed.
American ships, mostly from Boston, set up temporary
shop on their anchored boats, while the missions and
ranchos about Los Angeles hauled hides and tallow to
the cliffs and to the solitary adobe warehouse overlooking San Pedro Bay. Dana, visiting the port a number of times on a hide-trader, during the thirties, said
sailors everywhere called it "the hell of California,"
for at San Pedro they had to roll cargoes up the slippery
cliffs and carry hides down and over the kelp-covered
rocks.

1846
A Grant

When José and Juan Sepulveda petitioned Governor Pio Pico for a grant of Palos Verdes in May of
1846, a diseño or map of the ranch and of the Bay of
San Pedro was sent along with it.

This map was made by William Money, Los Angeles' eccentric No. 1, surveyor, philosopher, builder,
anatomist, cartographer, author and cult leader. It
showed ships in the harbor as well as houses of the
Sepulvedas and of Machado. It showed mountains and
ports and estuaries. It showed "Verdes" shortened to

Verde, in conformity with Money's ideas on spelling reform.

Pico issued his grant to José and Juan Sepulveda on June 3, 1846. A few days later Mayor Cota and two line-bearers marked the boundaries of Rancho Los Palos Verdes and officially gave possession to the grantees. The rift between the Sepulveda and Dominguez families was ended and ever since the members have been neighbors, friends and co-workers.

Both the Sepulveda and Dominguez families participated in the Mexican War. Ygnacio, one of the sons of the founder of the Sepulveda family, was killed at the Battle of La Mesa. Manuel Dominguez is said to have taken part in the Battle of Dominguez Ranch, fought on Rancho San Pedro, in which a bronze four-pounder (called the "Old Woman") was used with *1846-7*
War devastating effect on Captain Gillespie's American forces as they retreated from Los Angeles to San Pedro. The Americans killed were buried on Dead Man's Island, the conical peak that had loomed up before Cabrillo when he entered the Bay in 1542 and had since been used as an occasional burying place, finally to be removed in the interests of harbor development.

At Guadalupe Hidalgo, Mexico, the treaty between the American and Mexican governments was signed. *1848*
Treaty By it California became a part of the United States.

In October of 1852 Manuel Dominguez and other members of the Dominguez family filed their claim (with the Board of United States Land Commissioners) to Rancho San Pedro, and in November of the same year José Loreto Sepulveda and Juan Sepulveda petitioned for Rancho Los Palos Verdes.

Both claims were speedily confirmed by the Board and approved, on appeal, by the District Court.

The patent for Rancho San Pedro, containing over 43,000 acres and including the site of Wilmington, was issued on December 18, 1858, during President Buchanan's administration.

The Sepulvedas had to wait a long time for their final papers. As late as 1880 José was urging a cousin in Congress to use his influence in getting the patent through. On June 22, 1880, while Rutherford B. Hayes was president, the precious document finally was issued.

On a San Pedro bluff, not far from the Government's 500-vara reservation, Diego Sepulveda in the year 1853 put up a building for his own and his passengers' use, together with a small storehouse on the beach below the bluff. This was Sepulveda's Landing, the end of Diego's stage line. From here travelers from Los Angeles, ocean-bound, were rowed out to the anchored ship and were extremely lucky if a sandbar did not intervene, making them jump out into the water, thigh deep, to give the boat a long push.

1853 Sepulveda Stages

The Sepulveda stages, carrying passengers from Los Angeles, followed the old canyon road that passed the homes of the three Sepulveda brothers. Entering the Rancho Los Palos Verdes near its northeasterly corner the road curved between the hills on the right and the lakes on the left. Don Juan's home came first into view.

From its high location, near the present intersection of Gaffey and Anaheim Streets, it overlooked Machado Lake. The next to loom up was Don José's, on the right side of Gaffey Street, and then came Don Diego's place. Diego had been the last of the brothers to build, his large two-story adobe, with upper veranda, being erected in 1853. It and the two immense pepper trees in front of it were long a landmark. Today the site of this handsome home is occupied by a filling station at the corner of Channel and Gaffey Streets just back of the West Basin drydock.

When a harbor-bound stage swung by Don Diego's house, followed by its cloud of dust, the whole household waved it on its way and boys on horseback raced it to the Landing.

The Sepulveda stage line was sold to J. J. Tomlinson. Tomlinson became a rival of a man named Phineas Banning who had begun to do a freighting and passenger-carrying business from the old Mission warehouse.

For $12,000.00 Manuel Dominguez deeded twenty-four hundred acres of land on December 22, 1854, to three well-known southern Californians: B. D. Wilson, W. T. B. Sanford and J. G. Downey. It was carved out of the Rancho San Pedro and included two-thirds of what became Wilmington. To quote an early description, it fronted "on an estuary of the sea which enters from the port of San Pedro, commencing near some sunken barrels, near the line of Rancho of Los Palos Verdes."

Lieutenant Ord, who had been the first to map Los Angeles, surveyed these twenty-four hundred acres of slough land, for the purpose of the deed, and in 1855 prepared a survey and subdivision.

This document was recorded a few years later by Phineas Banning, Tomlinson's rival in staging, freighting, shipping and transportation. Banning, who had come to Los Angeles in 1851, bought a large interest in the Wilmington area and took the lead in planning a town at the head of the slough and building a wharf and warehouses.

With the new town as his terminal point, Banning had figured that the distance from Los Angeles to the waterfront would be shortened by six miles, and some hills would be avoided. Hitherto he had done business on the bluff at the old Mission warehouse, competing with Tomlinson who used Sepulveda's Landing.

For many years Banning's powerful figure, hearty manners and red suspenders loomed large on the San Pedro and Wilmington waterfronts.

Today visitors to Wilmington may drop in at the old Banning home, within a public park. They will carry away the memory of a three-story Colonial mansion, large stables, a garden estate, the whole bearing the impress of ample living.

On September 25, 1858, freight and passengers were landed for the first time at "San Pedro New Town," or "New San Pedro," as Wilmington was first called. An arm of the sea reaching inland, a channel deep enough to float barges and a steam tug to bring passengers and freight from and to anchored vessels, made the new port possible.

Following a partition made under court supervision in 1862, a new map, taking in new territory, was prepared. It was called "Map of New San Pedro" and showed the various blocks divided among Banning, Wilson, Myles, Downey, McFarland and Dominguez. This remains the official map of Wilmington and can be found among the County Recorder's records in Book 6, Pages 66 and 67 of Deeds.

In a few years New San Pedro gave way to "Wilmington," named after Wilmington, Delaware, Captain Banning's birthplace.

Wilmington grew slowly until the government stationed soldiers there during the Civil War and handled all the army supplies for southern California through that port. Camp Drum and Drum Barracks were established and prosperity hit the town, with travelers paying $1.50 to ride on Banning's tugs and shippers paying dearly for the haul out beyond Dead Man's Island. A camel express, planned in 1863, started from Drum Barracks with Tucson as destination.

In 1869 a railroad from Los Angeles to Wilmington was completed.

A breakwater was built between Rattlesnake Island and Dead Man's Island in 1871, creating a current in the channel which was dredged to a depth of seventeen or eighteen feet. This was done by the federal government. For the first time good-sized vessels could cross the bar at low tide.

*1871
Harbor
Beginnings*

(Rattlesnake Island is now Terminal Island, its original name having been given it because of the reptiles that once abounded, their number being increased, it is said, by winter floods that brought the rattlers down the San Gabriel River from the mountains.)

Jotham Bixby of Rancho Los Cerritos began buying interests in the Sepulveda grant as early as 1872, using the land as a cattle ranch. Other individuals acquired portions and fractional interests. A partition under court direction was in order and Rancho Los Palos Verdes, like many other Mexican ranches, was split among various claimants.

1872 Bixby Buys

In the partition decree, rendered in 1882, the largest parcel, half of the grant, went to Bixby. Bixby got seventeen thousand acres of rolling hills and sea cliffs, with fourteen miles of coast line. This is now the colorful and attractive Palos Verdes Estates.

About a dozen persons shared in the partition, with the Sepulveda heirs salvaging very little for themselves.

Accompanying the report upon the partition of the Rancho was the first official map of the little seaport town that clustered on the yellow bluffs above San Pedro Bay. It was made by Charles T. Healey and was filed with the County Clerk.

1882 Town of San Pedro

San Pedro, as shown on this first map, extended as far south as the old "Government Reserve" (now Fort MacArthur)—site of the lone warehouse of hide-trading days—and as far north as one block above First Street. Its west boundary was the street now called Pacific Avenue. The Southern Pacific Railroad Company's right of way was shown along the front, for railroad facilities had already been extended to San Pedro, causing commerce to leave Wilmington. Back of the right of way was the small plaza.

San Pedro was incorporated in February of 1888.

In April, 1908, a group of Los Angeles officials stood on a bluff overlooking San Pedro Bay. They saw what Dominguez, Sepulveda and Banning had seen many years before. But also, in imagination, they saw long miles of docks, warehouses, freight sheds, industrial plants—with the ships of the nations coming and going.

The first step toward making their vision a reality was the consolidation of San Pedro and Wilmington with Los Angeles. This was done on August 28, 1909.

1909
Union with
Los Angeles

The consolidation of two seaports with an inland metropolis gave Los Angeles frontage on the blue Pacific. Now, with the gift of tide and submerged lands from the State of California in 1911, municipal development of the harbor was possible. Henceforth, with her own funds and her own hands, Los Angeles could take full advantage of her direct contact with the sea and with world markets.

1911
A Gift of
Tide Lands

In 1871 the man-made harbor had been given its start when government money built the low rock jetty between Terminal Island and Dead Man's Island, the latter since removed. In the early nineties government aid brought about the dredging of a channel and in 1899 enabled the first load of quarried rock to be dropped into the ocean, beginning the eleven-thousand-foot breakwater that was completed in 1912.

In 1913 Los Angeles, owner of a port, voted the first bonds for harbor improvement.

Since then, under City control and operation by her Board of Harbor Commissioners, the harbor has reached the front rank of American ports, with a billion dollars worth of commerce flowing in and out each year.

A detached breakwater in the Outer Harbor, under construction since 1932, to be twelve thousand five hundred feet long when finished, will give new protection to ships and new importance to Los Angeles Harbor.

Out of the mud flats and the shallow waters that edged the ranchos of San Pedro and Los Palos Verdes a great harbor, man-made, has sprung to life.

Today

Today smooth highways wind toward the top of what Juan José Dominguez used to call "El Cerro de San Pedro," and from the heights we may look down upon a shining ocean, a harbor dark with wharfs, shipping and government craft, a city sloping to the water, other cities spreading inland and the haze of industrial smoke hanging over what, in a pastoral age, was the domain of Dominguez and Sepulveda.

Today, on a two-hour boat trip about Los Angeles Harbor, we see breakwaters, channels, docks, warehouses, lumber, fish canneries, oil tanks, vessels of the world and American battleships. We forget the old Bay of San Pedro where the Indians of Suanga launched canoes for Catalina, where Spanish galleons anchored, where foreign smugglers slipped in by night, where sailors from Boston toiled, the old Bay where, at spring-time, Juan José Dominguez and José Dolores Sepulveda watched blue waters stirred by countless spouting whales.

Don Julio Verdugo and His Flocks

GLENDALE

and the story of the
RANCHO SAN RAFAEL

SPANISH OCCUPATION of California began at San Diego in 1769, under the leadership of Gaspar de Portolá.

Among the soldiers sent north to San Diego was an ambitious young man named José Maria Verdugo. Verdugo was destined to become the owner of a thirty-six-thousand-acre California rancho and within the boundaries of his land was to arise the City of Glendale.

The date this soldier reached San Diego is not disclosed. Being a native of Loreto, Baja California, it is possible he enlisted—as did his brother, Mariano de la Luz—with the "leather-jackets" that marched north from Loreto in 1769 under Captain Rivera.

1769
Spaniards in California

More likely he came a little later. "The earliest mention of José Maria Verdugo in Alta California," says Thomas Workman Temple II, who has made an exhaustive search of mission and presidio records, "is on July 13, 1772, when he stood sponsor for an Indian baptized at San Carlos de Monterey Mission." Seven years later, at San Gabriel, young Verdugo married the daughter of Ygnacio Lopez, Maria de la Encarnacion.

Corporal Verdugo, on "detached" service at the Mission of San Gabriel, had some definite ideas about his own future, as well as good eyes for good land.

About a league and a half from the Mission on the road to Monterey lay a vast triangular tract, the southern tip of which pointed to the three-year-old Pueblo of Los Angeles and was the meeting of the Arroyo Seco (then called the Arroyo Hondo) and the Los Angeles River. Neither Mission nor Pueblo was using this land. It was called *Haleameupet* by the Indians whose brush huts clustered near the river and in the sycamore groves along the Arroyo.

Verdugo saw the broad, grass-covered acres that rolled back to the wooded hills on the north. In imagination he saw his own cattle pastured there, a water dam, similar to the Saca de Agua of the Pueblo, and irrigated fields.

He went direct to Governor Fages, his army commander, with a petition that he be allowed to keep his cattle and horses upon the favored tract. He mentioned, incidentally, that similar permission had been given another San Diego soldier, Juan José Dominguez, in connection with a place on the river south of the Mission and that the fortunate Dominguez was about to move with all his possessions.

The Governor, replying on October 20, 1784, said:

*1784
Verdugo's
Land*

"I concede to the petitioner the permission which he solicits to keep his cattle and horses at the Arroyo Hondo, distant a league and a half from the Mission of San Gabriel on the Monterey Road, provided that he does not prejudice the said Mission nor the inhabitants of the Reina de los Angeles, and, having some one in charge, without being exposed to the Gentile Indians or in any manner injuring them."

José Maria Verdugo, of the Royal Presidio of San Diego, did not give up his corporalship when, in 1784, he was allowed to establish himself on what was to become known as Rancho San Rafael.

He stayed with the army and sent his brother in his place to build a house (the first one was of "sticks"), plant a garden and a vineyard and look after his cattle and horses.

No detail was too small to be brought to the Governor's attention and in 1788 the archives disclose this order by Fages on the margin of a petition by José Mª Verdugo:

"In the Royal name of His Majesty I grant to the petitioner the use in right of ownership of the brand which he exhibits in order to mark his cattle."

By the year 1797, Verdugo had "five small girls and one small child," had become weary of the army and longed to retire to his rancho, where he had 200 head of horned cattle, 200 horses and 150 sheep—as well as crops produced with the aid of his water dam. On December 4 of that year, with the permission of his lieutenant, he wrote the Governor:

"I find myself much afflicted with dropsy, as is well known, for which reason, feeling myself entirely incapable for all duty as a sentinel or as a scout, I . . . solicit my retirement . . . I require some greater ease and cannot persuade myself that your Honor's compassion can deny me it . . ."

If he retired to one of the pueblos, Verdugo pointed out, he would have to suffer "the various fatigues in which all persons, although for good, share in common." But if he retired to "La Zanja," his name for Rancho San Rafael, he could join forces with his brother and a brother-in-law and make a good living.

From Monterey, Governor Borica, on January 12, 1798, gave his reply. Verdugo was allowed to retire and to establish himself as a rancher. Borica urged him, however, to improve the breed of his sheep and advised him not to prejudice the neighboring missions and to treat both Christian and Gentile Indians "with that love

*1798
Allowed
to Retire*

and charity so much recommended by the laws, but not for this to forbear living with the proper precaution, so as to avoid all insult."

Verdugo proceeded at once to the rancho where he was joined by his brother and—in place of the brother-in-law, who failed him—a Los Angeles friend of his, Antonio Rosa.

When cattle were being rounded up, the Arroyo Hondo had always been recognized as the dividing line between Verdugo's ranch and the lands of San Gabriel Mission.

But when a new priest arrived at the Mission in 1814 and ordered a sheep ranch to be established on the Verdugo side of the Arroyo, with corrals for the animals and huts for the Indian shepherds, the retired corporal appealed—as he always did—to the Governor. The Governor promptly "ordered the sheep to be taken away and they were taken away," thereby upholding the Arroyo Hondo as a boundary.

1814-17 Boundary Disputes

Over on the other side of the Verdugo ranch no one ever knew just where the ranch ended and the San Fernando Mission property began. Even during a rodeo the major-domo of the Mission would not remove cattle that had strolled over on the lands claimed by Verdugo. Furthermore, crops of Indian corn and beans were harvested, without Verdugo's knowledge, on what he supposed was his ranch.

Appeal was made to the Governor. Acting for him, the Alcalde of Los Angeles in 1817 sent forth representatives of both claimants who traveled horse-

back over the whole San Fernando Valley. With sycamores, hollow oaks and mounds of stones for markers,
they established a dividing line between the Mission's
Cahuenga Rancho and the Corporal's Rancho San
Rafael.

Meanwhile Verdugo was able to report progress in
ranch activities. On July 28, 1817, he made the following statement to the Governor as to the number of cattle
and horses then on the ranch:

Large cattle	1800
Small cattle	100
Wild horses	600
Gentle horses	70
Gentle mules	20
Wild mules	50

1817
Progress

Spanish control of California ended in 1822 but
there was no interruption in the way of living on
Rancho San Rafael. Spain, Mexico—it made little dif-
ference.

Ever since his "well known" dropsy made it important for him to retire from the army, Verdugo seems
not to have been in good health. Letters among the
old records bear this out, one being from his friend
Manuel Rodriguez, written on January 11, 1809, and
addressed to "The retired Corporal with the grade of
Sergeant, Joseph Mª Verdugo, at his rancho of San
Rafael." It read:

"Antonio Ygnacio Abila has delivered to me
the four cases of manteca . . . whose value of
fifty-five dollars, two reals, I leave credited to

your account. I regret your indisposition and
am glad you have felt some relief from the bleed-
ings, which in fact are very good for a pain in
the side—with fresh drinks taken moderately.
As respects your daughter Maria Antonia, it is
necessary for her to be resigned to the will of
God, asking for the intercession of His Most
Holy Mother for what may be suitable for her.
About the end of next February or the first of
March I shall necessarily need more manteca.
And, nothing else needful occurring, he desires
for you, your entire restoration to health."

On August 13, 1828, burdened with illness, José
Maria Verdugo summoned witnesses and signed his last
will and testament.

1828
Verdugo's
Will

"In the first place," he began, "I recommend
my soul to God, and it is my will that, with the
consent of our Father San Francisco, my body
be interred in the church of San Gabriel with
mass sung in the presence of the corpse . . . It
is my will that three novenas of mass be held
for me . . . It is my will that all my debts, legiti-
mately proving that they are correct, be paid."

(After listing the sums of money various persons
owed him for young bulls, fat cows and aguardiente
and declaring he himself owed no one, he made provision for his four children, Maria Antonia having
died. Catalina and Julio were the favored ones. Catalina was given cattle, horses, a 2-room house, furniture,
the granary, six and a half yoke of oxen and the vine-

yard. To Julio went pack saddles, a large still, pistols, shotguns, aguardiente and a small crucifix. Catalina and Julio each received half of the fruit trees. The will closes with a disposition of the rancho itself.)

"I declare that it is my will that the Rancho which the Nation granted to me, called San Rafael, be left to my son Julio and to Catalina, in order that they may enjoy the same with the blessing of God."

A year later, when Verdugo wished to add a few paragraphs, he could not sign his name. Julio did it for him. Still the old corporal lingered on.

Upon the death of José Maria Verdugo on April 12, 1831, the title to the Rancho San Rafael passed to Julio Verdugo and Catalina Verdugo.

1831
Death
Comes

Life on Rancho San Rafael was unaffected by the death of its first owner. There was a Mexican War in 1846 and California became a part of the United States in 1848. Still, life flowed on in leisurely course at the ranch, under the patriarchal management of Julio Verdugo, who was aided by his many sons. Julio had built himself a new home soon after the death of José Maria. In fact, he built several homes and huts, to accommodate the large family and for his own convenience when working his fields. He and his sons raised crops of barley, wheat, corn, beans and hay and they had large herds of cattle and horses. Many hides from San Rafael went down to San Pedro and thence by ship to New York and Boston.

Don Julio, himself, carrying on the traditions of his

father, rode horseback over his acreage and into the
Pueblo dressed in Spanish caballero fashion. The rest
of the family did not go in for display.

The Verdugo fiestas and rodeos are still remembered. Bears infested the canyons between the Glendale and Montrose regions. It is said that visitors, therefore, were met by vaqueros to give them safe escort
along Verdugo Road. The firing of guns and the waving of serapes kept away the wild beasts.

Catalina, Julio's sister, did not fare so well as her
brother. Blinded from an attack of smallpox, she was
destined to have no husband and to spend many years
visiting one after another of her nephews.

1851
The Land
Commission

A year after California was admitted as a State to
the Union in 1850, a Board of Land Commissioners was
created to investigate and pass upon land titles.

Julio and Catalina Verdugo filed their petition with
the Commission, basing their claim upon the two Spanish concessions made to their father in 1784 and 1798.

Their attorney was Joseph Lancaster Brent, an expert on land titles, who also represented Los Angeles
when it sought to have the Pueblo's title confirmed.
Brent gave Don Julio legal advice and also taught him
and his thirteen sons how to vote the straight Demo-
cratic ticket.

The Board confirmed the petitioners' title on September 11, 1855, and, on appeal, the United States
District Court upheld the Board.

It was many years, however, before the government had completed its survey, showing over 36,000 acres within the Rancho's boundaries.

The patent itself, signed by President Chester A. Arthur, was not issued until 1882.

The day after New Year's, in 1861, Julio Verdugo signed a document that was the beginning of the end of the Verdugos' ownership of Rancho San Rafael. It was a mortgage for $3,445.37 in favor of Jacob Elias who had advanced money for house-building, provisions, seeds and the payment of taxes. The note bore interest at 3% per month payable quarterly. In the mortgage the land covered was described as bounded on the north by the Sierra Madre, on the east by the Arroyo Hondo, on the south by the Los Angeles River and on the west by the lands of Jonathan R. Scott, cultivated by him, excepting only the portions that had been sold to J. D. Hunter and J. L. Brent.

*1861
A
Mortgage*

The other great event of the year was the partition of the rancho between Julio and Catalina, in accordance with the wishes of their father. A line was drawn from a point on the easterly side of the river, opposite the house of Antonio Feliz, and extended northeasterly and easterly to Piedra Gorda (now called Eagle Rock) and to the Arroyo Seco. Catalina took the land north of this line, a region of mountains, canyons and young streams, a country abounding in willows, sycamores and oaks. She was never to see its beauty, but at the adobe house of her brother's son, Teodoro, in Verdugo Canyon, she could be comfortable for the rest of her life.

Julio took the land south of the dividing line. Within his land most of Glendale was to arise.

1869
Sheriff's
Sale

At ten o'clock on March 8th of 1869, Sheriff Burns
offered at public auction the property that had been
mortgaged to Jacob Elias. Eight years of mounting
debt, built up by interest rates that were customary but
ruinous, had brought the $3,445.37 up to $58,750.00
and with it foreclosure and ruin to the son of the
retired corporal of the Royal Presidio of San Diego.

Alfred B. Chapman was the purchaser at the sheriff's
auction sale, his bid being the amount of the debt. Six
months later the sheriff gave him a deed.

Julio did not entirely lose out, however, as Chapman almost immediately quitclaimed back two hundred
acres, located so as to take in the home place.

Conveyances to creditors and lawyers by Julio of
portions of his two hundred-acre homestead, by Catalina of various undivided interests and by their successors in title made inevitable a division or partition under
court direction.

When the referees and surveyors had completed
their work, the Ranchos San Rafael and La Cañada
were so carved up that the retired corporal would never
have recognized the region that had once been his
domain. There were twenty or more allottees and
twice that many allotments.

Among the Verdugos, Catalina, Teodoro, Rafaela
Verdugo de Sepulveda, Maria Sepulveda de Sanchez
and Julio received substantial parcels, the largest of
which was over 2500 acres in extent. Julio's 200-acre

place was recognized. Other members of the family received tiny slices.

Sharing in the partition were Benjamin Dreyfus— receiving the largest parcel, nearly 8500 acres—Prudent Beaudry, Alfred B. Chapman, Andrew Glassell, O. W. Childs and Captain C. E. Thom. *1871 Partition*

On lands awarded to the last four named men was to arise a new town: Glendale.

Catalina Verdugo died in 1871, the year of the partition, and Julio Verdugo in 1876. Catalina's last days were spent with Teodoro, her favorite nephew, who took care of her, although he had a large family of his own. Teodoro's adobe still stands, a small, pleasant place in Verdugo Canyon. Julio's home, for the last seven years of his life, was the adobe of his wife at Porto Suelo.

After the partition Rancho San Rafael was not a Verdugo ranch. What was left to the Verdugo family was to melt away before the invasion of creditors and newcomers. The various adobes that dotted the great ranch were to tumble into ruin and oblivion, except those of Teodoro and of Maria Sepulveda de Sanchez. The latter's place, built on a hundred-acre tract which Maria received in 1872 from Rafaela on a trade of the Sanchez allotment, may be seen today at 1340 Dorothy Drive. It is municipally owned and has been successfully restored: an example of a simple, early California ranch house set in a garden true to type.

Following the partition of the Verdugo ranch, newcomers began to drift in, attracted by the good soil, the climate and the superb setting. They bought large tracts, built homes, planted fruit orchards—citrus, peach, prune, apricot—and became the pioneers of modern Glendale. The names of Patterson, Byram, Crow, Phelon, Ross, Bullis, Bachman, Cook, Sherer, Morgan, Hodgkins, Woolsey, Hayes, Dunsmoor, Luckens, Woodbury and Rivers are of this period. With them should be listed M. L. Wicks, early subdivider, and the other two members of his firm, C. H. Watts and E. T. Wright.

1886
Newcomers

With a real estate boom in sight, several of these pioneers pooled portions of their lands and platted a townsite. Captain C. E. Thom was one of them. He had been a Confederate officer and after the Civil War resumed his law practice in Los Angeles, investing his funds in Rancho San Rafael real estate. His nephew, Erskine M. Ross, was another of the founders of Glendale, a former Confederate officer also and destined to go far in the legal profession. In 1883 Judge Ross built a large residence on his ranch which he called "Rossmoyne." A third to join in with the subdividers was Harry J. Crow, whose large acreage lay west of Glendale Avenue and south of Broadway. Crow is remembered also as the planter of the Lomita Avenue eucalyptus trees. B. F. Patterson and E. T. Byram, who purchased part of the O. W. Childs allotment after the partition, were active in the plans for the new town.

1887
Town of
Glendale

In January of 1887 the survey was completed and on March 11 the map of the "Town of Glendale" was recorded in the office of the County Recorder.

The boundaries were First Street (now Lexington Drive) on the north, Sixth (now Colorado) Street on the south, Central Avenue on the west and what is now Chevy Chase Drive on the east.

The name of "Glendale" was older than its plat. It had been adopted at a school-house meeting of all the people in the valley, in 1884, winning out over Verdugo, San Rafael, Porto Suelo, Riverdale, Etheldean and Minneapolis.

While Glendale was getting under way a rival town was started a little to the south. This was Tropico, destined finally, in 1918, to be consolidated with the northern city.

When the Great Boom of the Eighties swept over southern California, Glendale, like a dozen other new towns, absorbed some of the influx of buyers, builders and settlers, though Glendale, an old settled community, was hardly a boom town. The subdividers had brought a dummy-engine line in from Los Angeles. The Glendale Improvement Society was organized. To keep up with other towns, a huge hotel was erected. A newspaper was started.

In 1888 the boom burst. Deflated towns littered the landscape and Glendale was one of them. The ornate but empty Glendale Hotel, that had not had time to be a hotel, loomed up over the tree-tops as if to symbolize the disaster.

1888 Boom Bursts

With Dr. D. H. Hunt as President and E. D. Goode as Secretary, the Glendale Improvement Society, dead since boom days, was revived in 1902.

Henceforth the City took on new life. The qualities of Glendale were advertised, new business was developed, new schools were built and people were encouraged to come in and make their homes on the glamorous Rancho San Rafael.

The most important act was the appointment of a railroad committee.

On July 2, 1904, a barbecue feast was held in Glendale. The beeves were prepared by a Mexican expert. The pickles came in barrels. There was food for everybody and all the coffee, lemonade and speeches that the citizens could absorb.

1904
Barbecue

The occasion was the extension of the Pacific Electric Railway system into Glendale, for which both Tropico and Glendale had worked.

To Leslie C. Brand, whose contributions and activities for the development of Glendale were to be many, goes chief credit for bringing the railroad into the old rancho and toward the Verdugo Mountains.

The chairman of the barbecue celebration was J. C. Sherer, later to become Glendale's chief historian. To the crowd he said:

"Yesterday Tropico celebrated and today we celebrate. If I could look into the future with an eye to prophecy I would say that tomorrow Burbank may celebrate, and possibly the next day San Fernando, and eventually La Canada, for I cannot believe that the road will stop here while just beyond us lies as beautiful a country just as fertile and populous, and, like

Glendale, waiting an outlet and an electric railway system to tie it to the world."

The village decided to become a city in 1906.

The railway, linking Glendale with all of southern
California, was bringing in people, a new business
center was being established and all was well with those
who were living upon the domain of José Maria Verdugo.

Henceforth, population figures were such a source
of pride that ultimately Glendale's slogan became:
"The fastest growing city in America."

For many years one of the pleasant features of the
City's life was the "Casa Verdugo," a restaurant managed by Señora Piedad Yorba de Sowl. The adobe
and shaded grounds that had been the home of Fernando Sepulveda, son-in-law of Julio Verdugo and
husband of Rafaela, stood at the end of the Pacific
Electric Railway and near the base of the Verdugo
Mountains. This place became one of the most popular dining-out spots in southern California. The Spanish dishes, the California wines, and the songs and
dancing of señoritas are remembered by those who
prefer to forget that the 1910 population of Glendale
was 2700 and that of 1920, 13,500.

*Not many of the seventy-five thousand people
who live in the Glendale of 1939, with its wide boulevards and its charming homes in valley and on hillside, can remember when its only roads were the
Verdugo, the San Fernando and the old highway lead-*

ing by the Sepulveda and Sanchez adobes. Few recall the scattered frame houses, the fields and the orchards of the handful of pioneers who then lived in the region. But everyone who enjoys thinking of the past may see, in imagination, Verdugo horsemen riding through great herds at rodeo-time and, farther away, the old corporal, José Maria Verdugo, summoning to his deathbed Julio and Catalina and bestowing upon them Rancho San Rafael "in order that they may enjoy the same with the blessing of God."

"Never a foot-print except the few we made"

LONG BEACH

and the story of the
RANCHO LOS ALAMITOS
and the
RANCHO LOS CERRITOS

WHEN WHITE MEN first came to live in California the site of Long Beach was a six-mile stretch of wide, magnificent beach, dotted at the water's edge with amber kelp and sea shells and covered near the palisades with yellow sand verbena, ice plant and sea figs; and, back of the palisades, an immense grassy plain.

49

There were Indians in this area, those of the village of Puvu located at the spring among the little cottonwoods (los alamitos) back of Alamitos Bay, and others from Suanga, near San Pedro's Inner Bay.

Long Beach was included within the land conceded in 1784 to a soldier as a place to graze his cattle. Like Dominguez and Verdugo, this soldier had campaigned under Governor Fages. He was Manuel Nieto, the third of California's three musketeers, whose claim originally extended from the Santa Ana River to the San Gabriel River and from the San Diego-San Gabriel Road to the sea. Later it was to be reduced, at the request of the Mission fathers, and finally to be split into five ranchos aggregating a hundred and fifty-eight thousand acres.

"I knew Manuel Nieto," was Felipe Talamantes' testimony before the United States Land Commission. "I was in his employ. I lived with him about two years. He had a house on the land in which he lived with his family. He had great numbers of cattle and horses, fifteen or twenty thousand or more. He had corrals and cultivated land. Nieto was an old man when he retired from the service."

The house Manuel Nieto built was southwest of the present Whittier, in what is now known as Los Nietos. The land he cultivated was close by his adobe. He never lived within the boundaries or vicinity of Long Beach.

When old Nieto died, in 1804, his children stayed

on the ranch. They divided their inheritance. Juan José, a son, got Los Alamitos, and Manuela, a daughter, the adjoining Los Cerritos. In these two ranchos lies the city of Long Beach, the ranch dividing line being Alamitos Avenue.

At a very early date Juan José Nieto took over Los Alamitos. He built his home on the brow of the hill where now stands Fred H. Bixby's ranch house. (On Anaheim Street east of the Long Beach Municipal Golf Links.) It overlooked the ancient spring—which had attracted the Indians—and a jungle of cottonwoods.

José Antonio Carrillo recalled going to this place about the year 1807.

"When I was quite a young man, about forty-five years ago," said Carrillo (in 1852), "I was at the house of Juan José. At his request I wrote a letter for him to the priest of the Mission of San Gabriel notifying him to take away some sheep from the said Juan José Nieto's land."

1807 Carrillo's Visit

José Castro was another eminent Californian who remembered visiting Los Alamitos, this time in 1821.

"He (Nieto) had on it about eight or nine thousand head of cattle, he had on it three or four large houses, one very large corral and another smaller one, some of the land enclosed and under cultivation. Juan José Nieto lived on it a long time and according to accounts he lived on it before I was born and continued to live on it until he sold it to Figueroa."

Castro was a twelve-year-old boy at the time of this visit.

In 1833 and 1834 the Mexican government confirmed the titles to Rancho Los Alamitos (the little cottonwoods) and to Rancho Los Cerritos (the little hills, having reference to Signal Hill and other knolls). It granted the former to Juan José Nieto. It granted the latter to Manuela Nieto (de Cota). Rancho Los Alamitos lies southeasterly of the present Alamitos Avenue, and Rancho Los Cerritos northwesterly. Most of Long Beach is within Los Cerritos.

1834
The
Governor

For five hundred dollars in cash Juan José Nieto sold his great ranch to José Figueroa, governor of California. The deed itself was dated June 30, 1834.

Governor Figueroa never lived on Los Alamitos. He put José Justo Morrillo in charge as superintendent. On Figueroa's death, which took place in Monterey in September of 1835, his brother and sole heir, Francisco, joined Morrillo. They remained in charge until the property could be sold in the administration of the estate.

The buyer was Abel Stearns, a shrewd Yankee from Salem, Massachusetts, who had come to Los Angeles and taken out Mexican citizenship. The deed for Los Alamitos was issued him on July 12, 1842. In

1842
Abel
Stearns

turning over the ranch, Francisco Figueroa made an inventory, listing horses, mules, hogs, sheep, cattle and also:

> "One house of adobe with two apartments covered with pitch and others without roof with two opposite doors. One more house of adobe with three apartments covered by rushes and

with one door placed therein. One other house of adobe with two apartments covered by rushes and with one door."

Rancho Los Alamitos made a pleasant summer home for Stearns' wife, who was the lovely Arcadia Bandini.

Rancho Los Cerritos also passed to Yankee hands. Its new owner was John Temple who had come to Los Angeles in 1827 and, like Stearns, taken out citizenship papers. He had married Rafaela Cota, daughter of Doña Manuela Nieto de Cota. Rafaela was one of the twelve children and heirs of the owner of Los Cerritos. Temple bought out the brothers and sisters of his wife, for about $3000 in silver, and became a ranchero. Judicial possession was given him in December of 1843.

1843 John Temple

He began building a ranch house near the Cota home, but not as close to the river. It is the stately house that stills stands, after a recent restoration, near the Virginia Country Club grounds. For its foundation Temple used bricks brought around the Horn. For its beams and floors he got hand-hewn redwood. For its walls there was sun-dried adobe, made on the premises, into which straw had been tramped by Indian feet. Upon the flat roofs there was poured hot asphaltum from the tar pits of Rancho La Brea. Temple also laid out an extensive garden.

From the ranch house of Los Cerritos John Temple governed his domain, upon which he pastured fifteen thousand cattle, seven thousand sheep and three thousand horses.

Stearns and Temple were neighbors and friendly rivals, the only ranch owners in the whole Long Beach area. On each rancho there were barbecues and rodeos, and on these occasions many a cask of wine was opened. Annually there was horse-racing between the two establishments, the race course being from El Cerrito (Signal Hill) straight to the beach.

1851
Land
Titles

Three years after California had been ceded to the United States by Mexico a Board of Land Commissioners was created by the government to investigate and pass upon the titles to land held or claimed.

John Temple's title to Rancho Los Cerritos was confirmed by the Board in 1853, and Abel Stearns' title to Rancho Los Alamitos in 1855. In both instances, on appeal to the United States District Court, a second confirmation was obtained. A patent for twenty-seven thousand acres of land was issued Temple in 1867 and one for twenty-eight thousand acres to Stearns in 1874.

The drought of the early sixties caused the death of thousands of cattle and, for the time being, ended happy days on the two ranches. Both owners lost their ranches. Temple had to sell and Stearns was foreclosed.

1866
Flints
and Bixbys

For $20,000 the lands and herds of Los Cerritos were bought by Benjamin and Thomas Flint and Llewellyn Bixby in 1866. A younger brother of Llewellyn, Jotham, was made ranch manager. Jotham Bixby later, in 1869, got a half interest.

The Flints and Bixbys were successful sheepmen and landowners from the northern part of the state who

had come to California from Maine during the gold
fever.

When Jotham moved into the hacienda that had
been Temple's he began stocking the ranch with sheep.
Wool-growing was to become its chief activity.

Los Alamitos meanwhile had gone to Michael Reese,
San Francisco money lender. Reese foreclosed the
mortgage which Stearns put on the ranch to complete
the building of his Arcadia Block in Los Angeles.
Jotham's cousin from Maine, John W. Bixby, leased
a portion of Los Alamitos in 1878. He and his wife
(Susan Hathaway) and their small son Fred moved
into the old ranch house. Before the lease ran out the
whole rancho was purchased from the heirs of Reese.
That was in the year 1881. Jotham Bixby and I. W.
Hellman shared with John W. Bixby in this purchase.

*1878
A Lease*

John W. Bixby's first step had been to put in order
the old adobe buildings that had been falling into ruin
since the days of Arcadia Bandini de Stearns and to
dispossess the rats. The ranch house stands today as
one of the most attractive country homes in the state,
surrounded by gardens and trees, the center of Fred
H. Bixby's active stock ranch.

So the whole of what is now Long Beach came into
the Bixby family, with the two ranchos devoted to
sheep-raising.

Sarah Bixby Smith, whose "Adobe Days" gave so
pleasant a picture of life on Los Cerritos and Los Alamitos, looked back upon this period and wrote, in 1925:

"Now the sheep are all gone, and the shearers and dippers are gone too. The pastoral life gave way to the agricultural, and that in turn to the town and city. There is Long Beach. Once it was a cattle range, then sheep pasture, then, when I first knew it, a barley field with one small house and shed standing about where Pine and First Streets cross. And the beach was our own private, wonderful beach . . . Nobody knows what a wide, smooth, long beach it was. There were gulls and many little shore birds, and never a foot-print except the few we made, only to be washed away by the next tide. Two or three times a summer we would go over from the ranch for a day, and beautiful days we had, racing on the sand, or going into the breakers with father or Uncle Jotham who are now thought of only as old men, venerable fathers of the city. Ying would put us up a most generous lunch, but the thing that was most characteristic and which is remembered best is the meat broiled over the little driftwood fire . . . I wonder if the chef of the fashionable Hotel Virginia, which occupies the site of our outdoors kitchen, ever served the guests so good a meal as we had on the sand of the beautiful, empty beach."

The first name of the town was not Long Beach, but Willmore—after William Erwin Willmore, whose plan it was. Willmore was an Englishman who had come to America in 1855.

Landing at Wilmington, California, one day in 1870, he set out on foot for Anaheim, following what is now Anaheim Street.

Near the spot where American Avenue now crosses Anaheim Street he stopped to rest and to admire the expanse of grass-covered plain. It occurred to him that here was a spot to establish a colony. With that thought the present Long Beach was born.

1870
*Willmore's
Plans*

Ten years later he took steps to carry out his colony dream. He secured an option from Jotham Bixby on four thousand acres that included the heart of present-day Long Beach. He organized the "American Colony," with plans to sell, at low prices, five, ten, twenty and forty acre farms to colonists who, with the aid of artesian wells, would raise oranges, lemons, figs, olives, almonds, walnuts, and would also indulge in dairy farming. He planned Willmore City and filed the first survey and subdivision with the County Clerk December 5, 1882. He advertised throughout the nation.

1882
*Willmore
City*

Finally sixty excursionists started from Kansas City, reached Los Angeles and Willmore City, drew up optimistic resolutions, but bought few lots. At the end of two years there were only about a dozen houses.

For lack of buyers Willmore's plans collapsed and the option was relinquished in 1884. The outlines of Long Beach, however, remained, with its present streets and Pacific Park. The highways that Mr. Willmore created still exist and were eighty feet wide, with the exception of Magnolia, Pacific, Atlantic and California which were one hundred feet and American which was one hundred and twenty-four feet in width.

When Willmore gave up his colonization fight the Long Beach Land and Water Company was organized by a new group of men: R. M. Widney, George Bonebrake, Thomas Mott, F. C. Howes and A. M. Hough. They took up where Willmore left off and went ahead with new plans, new money and a new name: "Long Beach." Pomeroy & Mills were their agents. They recorded the official map of the present Long Beach July 30, 1887.

1887
Long
Beach

From then on there has been no turning back. The boom of the Eighties swept over southern California and Long Beach, like other places, won recognition and became an established seaside resort.

As early as 1888 it could be said of Long Beach in the Lindley and Widney guide-book, "California of the South":

"Long Beach is a delightful sea-side resort twenty-three miles from Los Angeles on the Wilmington branch of the Southern Pacific Railroad. There are several trains daily. Long Beach contains elegant hotels, a large Methodist Episcopal church, a Congregational church, good public schools, stores and livery-stables, but no saloons. Herein is one great point in which it differs from Santa Monica. In the latter place there are to be found all classes of society, from the veriest hoodlum to the most reputable citizen; but in Long Beach no saloons are tolerated, and all objectionable elements of society are kept out.

"The social life at Long Beach is of a kind that most delights people of refined tastes. There is nothing loud; there is much that is esthetic. It is, par excellence, an educational wateringplace . . . The Chautaqua Assembly has its annual meeting here every summer . . . The beach is a perfect natural race-course, and during the season spanking teams from the city can always be seen dashing over this superb driveway."

The Terminal Railroad in 1891 gave direct tourist and freight connections with Los Angeles, but when the Pacific Electric built to Long Beach in 1902 the city's population began to increase tremendously. By 1910 there were eighteen thousand people and by 1920 fifty-five thousand. Long Beach's climate and superb sea-bathing made it a favorite summer resort for the Southwest. And so popular was it among the people of the Middle West that it gained the title of "Seacoast of Iowa."

1902 People Come

By legislative act, approved May 1, 1911, the State of California granted to the City of Long Beach tide lands and submerged lands bordering upon and below the mean high tide line. A similar act was passed and approved in 1925 which took care of tide lands bordering upon the enlarged boundary of the city.

1911 Tide Lands

These acts have made harbor development possible. The Long Beach-Los Angeles Harbor came into being. And in 1928 the citizens approved a bond issue that created the Rainbow Pier—a pier and breakwater extending fourteen hundred feet from the shore line, between Pine and Linden Avenues—and a handsome Municipal Auditorium.

The discovery in 1921 of oil at Signal Hill made the ownership, production and sale of oil the most important activity of the city—for the time being. By 1922 the Signal Hill fields, former scene of horse races between the Temple and Stearns families, were producing more than two hundred and fifty thousand barrels a day. The population of Long Beach soon leaped to more than one hundred thousand.

1921
Oil at
Signal Hill

Over the old ranchos of Los Cerritos and Los Alamitos—both owned a few years ago by one family—a city of a hundred and seventy-two thousand people has spread an intricate pattern. Seaside resort, shipping and industrial center, Long Beach has built at lusty speed. Its earthquake of 1933 gave it a new stride. Its homes and buildings have taken the cattle range, the sheep pasture and the barley field of the Nieto-Cota-Stearns-Temple-Bixby eras. Signal Hill and nearby knolls—los cerritos—bristle with oil derricks. Hotels and apartment houses crowd the palisades. The wide, white beach that gave the city a name has spawned an amusement zone—the Pike—smelling of popcorn, hot dogs and sea air, the lure for sailors, inland Cali-

Today

fornians, ocean-hungry Oklahomans and curious east-
erners. The surf pounds in and a medley of bathers
make merry. Offshore, ride at anchor the gray battleships, the aircraft carriers and the sleek cruisers of the
United States Fleet. Long Beach, with its horse-shoe
pitching, churches, roller-coasters, checker players, con-
ventions, oil workers, auctions, lectures, band concerts,
old-time dances, banks, giant Sunday-school classes,
fortune tellers, golf courses, new homes, sun-bathers,
modern schools, water carnivals, parks and Iowa picnics
—Long Beach has swallowed the Ranchos Los Cerritos
and Los Alamitos.

When Whittier Was a Barley Field

WHITTIER

and the story of the
RANCHO PASO DE BARTOLO VIEJO

THE SITE OF WHITTIER before white men came was an unoccupied slope at the western end of the rolling Puente Hills. Live oaks dotted the hillsides. Sycamores marked the course of the arroyos, including Turnbull Canyon, that came down over the high land to meet the San Gabriel River hidden by green willows. Between hills and river were several tiny lakes.

62

Near the river were brush huts, the dwellings of Indians who lived on wild seeds, small game and honey. This was the village of *Sejat*, so called by Father Boscana of San Juan Capistrano. It was the traditional "place of wild bees," whose hives were located in holes found in the river banks. Long ago the people of the village became too many in number. Some of them wandered south and colonized the Valley of San Juan Capistrano. The story of the journey from the Whittier region passed into the writings of Geronimo Boscana.

Before 1769
Place of
Wild Bees

Sejat, sometimes called *Suka*, may have been at the knoll of black sandy soil a short distance downstream from the Pio Pico mansion. It may have been near the Southern Pacific Junction Tower that stands at the crossing of the Whittier spur of the Southern Pacific with the Santa Fe or near the Tomas Sanchez Colima house—at both of which spots were Indian graveyards. Its site may have been just west of the old Guirado place where the first white settler, José Manuel Nieto, built his home. John P. Harrington, Indian authority, suggests these places for they were pointed out to him by Juan Ramirez who had lived eighty years in this region.

All of these people of the Indian past, however, must have found the Whittier slope too far from the river for a dwelling place. It was good for rabbit hunting. It was a region to cross when going back into the hills and to the springs in Turnbull Canyon, and for the Indian boys who wished to catch a glimpse of the ocean it was worth a walk up from the river.

From the beginnings of San Gabriel Mission (in

1771) on the other side of the hills until the years 1833-1834, when secularization laws were enforced, all of the Whittier section came under the Mission's jurisdiction.

An ex-soldier named José Manuel Nieto, often called Manuel Nieto, received a concession or permit to put his cattle on what came to be called Rancho Los Nietos. This was when the Pueblo of Los Angeles was about three years old.

1784
Nieto's
Concession

With his cattle he went into possession of a small portion of a vast acreage that included part of Whittier.

"Nieto's house was an adobe hut about twenty feet square," said the late Allin L. Rhodes, who interviewed the aged widow of Manuel Nieto's grandson, Diego Nieto. "It stood a quarter of a mile south of what came to be known as Carpenter's Lane and immediately west of the Bernardino Guirado place."

Other white men and their families settled along the river and even before the year 1800 "the place of wild bees" was patterned with fields where Indian servants worked.

Manuel Nieto died in 1804, but his adobe home stood until washed away by the floods that came raging through the vineyards and cornfields in 1867. The family of Lemuel Carpenter owned and occupied it at the time of its destruction.

Nieto's three-hundred-thousand-acre claim of land had long before been reduced, at the request of Mission authorities. Finally it had been broken up into five ranchos and granted to heirs or successors of Nieto. In none of these was Whittier included. The Santa Gertrudes Rancho, whose boundaries touch Whittier on the south and within whose area the Nieto homestead had been located, was the most northerly of the five.

When California became Mexican, in 1822, the Whittier area still lay in the center of, but apart from, the activities of soldiers, priests and settlers.

El Camino Real came from La Habra, forming the northeast boundary of the Rancho Santa Gertrudes, identifying itself in part with the present Whittier Boulevard, crossing the river, thence to the Mission San Gabriel, finally reaching the Pueblo of Los Angeles. It was the main highway connecting missions and presidios from San Diego to San Francisco.

1822
El Camino
Real

When a member of the Yorba family from Rancho Santiago de Santa Ana wished to go to the Pueblo, he followed Whittier Boulevard part of the way. If a priest at San Juan Capistrano wanted to visit his friends at San Gabriel, his horse kept to the road that became the southwest boundary of Whittier. A farmer of Los Nietos went to town by the same way. Cattle and men on horseback raised clouds of dust through a region that is now green with orange groves.

One of the early settlers on Los Nietos ranch had been Juan Crispin Perez. In September of 1833 he petitioned the authorities for a grant of his own.

San Gabriel—in the midst of secularization—offered no objections, nor did the Pueblo of Los Angeles object.

Investigation by the Los Angeles Ayuntamiento or Council showed that, with the consent of the Nieto family, Perez had been keeping his cattle "for the space of thirty years a little more or less" on the tract the title to which he sought.

1835
The Grant
to Perez

On June 12, 1835, Governor Figueroa granted Perez a ranch, the Paso de Bartolo Viejo. Old maps show it as adjoining the Santa Gertrudes Rancho on the north, and extending between the Puente Hills and the river, thus including all of Whittier.

Eventually the Perez claim was cut down by the United States Land Commission until most of Whittier was excluded. No part of this grant, as finally patented in 1881, lies in the original "townsite" of Whittier. Only sixteen and a half acres of it lies within the surrounding area originally subdivided by the founders. Later growth, however, to the north of Whittier Boulevard and to the west of Citrus Avenue, has brought into the city much more of the rancho.

During these years, when land titles were in dispute, sheepherders drove their flocks over the Puente Hills, camping at the springs in Turnbull Canyon.

At Paso de Bartolo on the San Gabriel River, whence came the name of the rancho, one battle of the struggle between Californians and Americans was fought, each side losing two dead and eight wounded. That was on January 8, 1847.

California was admitted to the Union as a state two years after it had been ceded to the United States by Mexico.

Pico, last Mexican governor of California, had fled to Mexico in 1846 when he saw opposition to the Americans was useless. A few months after the signing of the Treaty of Guadalupe Hidalgo, however, he returned to become a loyal American and to become a character in Whittier's story.

Between August of 1850 and March of 1852 he paid a total of $4642 to the children of Perez—who had died in March or April of 1847—and to Bernardino Lopez who had succeeded to the widow's interest. In return he received four deeds. Juan Perez, another heir, some years later also made Pico a deed.

"On the decease of Juan Crispin Perez in 1847," said Hugo Reid, in a deposition made on November 4, 1852, before the United States Land Commission, "the land continued in the occupation of his heirs. It is now occupied by Pio Pico. He has built a house on it in which he lives and has stock on it."

1850-52
El
Ranchito

Pico affectionately called his place "El Ranchito" because it was so small. It contained only nine thousand acres, whereas his Santa Margarita y Las Flores in San Diego County had one hundred and thirty-three thousand acres.

Don Pio went in for gaming, horse races and hospitality. At his home he and his fortunate guests dined in the patio that faced the Puente Hills and danced in the ballroom that opened toward the river.

Floods in the year 1867 brought the San Gabriel raging through his orchards and up to the walls of his adobe mansion. The storm waters followed Pico's large irrigating ditch and created the present channel. The bed of the Rio Hondo of today was the San Gabriel's former channel.

Pico was much interested in Whittier which he watched rise at the base of the Puente Hills in the late Eighties. On the streets of the town his stocky figure, his velvet coat and his heavy jewelry were often seen and commented upon.

Until a few years before his death in 1894 Pio Pico lived at "El Ranchito." Creditors finally took his last possession and forced him out.

The greater portion of the site of Whittier became public land when it was excluded from the final survey of Rancho Paso de Bartolo Viejo.

1868
Farmer
Gerkins

A German farmer named Jacob F. Gerkins came to Los Angeles in 1854, filed a claim under the homestead laws on December 2, 1868, to the northeast quarter of Section 21, Township 2 South, Range 11 West. This quarter section—one hundred and sixty acres— today lies just north of Hadley Street and east of Greenleaf Avenue. It was the nucleus of the "Thomas Ranch" that later was to be bought by the founders of Whittier.

The United States did not issue its patent to Gerkins until the middle of 1874, three and a half years after he had sold out his interest.

Following Gerkins' example, other individuals and organizations took title to the balance of the original Whittier area—either by patent from the United States or from the State of California. The State had selected part of this region in place of "school sections" allotted to it.

Through purchase and foreclosure during the years 1880 and 1881 it came into the hands of one man, John M. Thomas, an Indiana farmer, who had come to California in 1859 and to Los Angeles in 1868.

1880-81
Thomas
Ranch

The Thomas Ranch became a landmark. A man making the two and three-quarter-hour drive from Los Angeles across the wide plain that is Montebello could look up to the brown Puente Hills and see at the base a green patch of trees near the Turnbull arroyo. These were pepper trees surrounding the home of Thomas, from whence he conducted his barley ranch.

A simple frame structure in the mid-western style, the Thomas house is Whittier's first building. It still stands—at 522 East Camilla Street—and is occupied by Mr. and Mrs. George G. Hunnicutt. Mrs. Hunnicutt is the granddaughter of Jonathan Bailey, Whittier's first citizen, who moved into the house when the ranch was sold to the founders of the city.

Some of the original pepper trees are left, to remind the owners of the time when a white sheet hung against one of them could be seen from Los Angeles through a telescope. In early days the occupants of the house used to signal by this method to relatives living on Hill Street in Los Angeles.

Thomas' 1275 acres came to be known as the "Mustard Ranch," for in early spring the mustard grew as high as a man on horseback.

In August of 1886 John M. Thomas gave up his
ranch. He deeded it to three individuals, J. Mills Boal,
James R. Boal and John D. Burch, the consideration
being $33,000.00.

While this was happening in California, Acquilla H.
Pickering in Chicago was completing plans for estab-
lishing an ideal community on the Pacific Coast.

1886-7
Pickering

Pickering was active in the Society of Friends and
during 1886 was busy answering questions from
Quakers who wanted to become colonists.

Early in the following year Pickering and his wife,
Hannah, were sent out to California to select a site
in the promised land. They traveled beyond Sacra-
mento on the north and as far as Ensenada, Lower
California, on the south. For three months they
searched.

One day they were taken on a drive through East
Los Angeles, out over the wide mesa, crossing the Rio
Hondo and the San Gabriel, passing between the Pico
Mansion and the little settlement of Jimtown and con-
tinuing up toward the high ground where pepper trees
marked the Thomas Ranch.

They proceeded on to the ranch house and the
hills. Looking back, they saw the whole valley and
far away the ocean.

The ranch was for sale and Pickering was much
pleased with it. He decided that a council of southern
California Friends should be called at once.

On May 3, 1887, the Thomas Ranch was purchased
by the Pickering Land and Water Company, of which

Jonathan Bailey was President, John Painter Vice-President and Hervey Lindley Secretary.

1887
A Town
is Born

Whittier had already been selected as the name for the new community, after the New England Quaker poet, John Greenleaf Whittier.

On May 11th Jonathan Bailey and his wife, Rebecca, established their home in the old ranch house among the pepper trees, thus becoming Whittier's first citizens. Four days later was Sunday and the Baileys held religious services on the front porch. Anyone who cared to attend was welcome at Whittier's first "meeting house." The bench on which the worshippers sat is still on the same front porch.

The survey and subdivision had been rushed and by the end of May the sale of lots started. Town lots were $100 to $200 and five-acre lots outside of the townsite were offered at $1000 each.

Meanwhile the Boom of the Eighties was sweeping over southern California. It caught up Whittier and presently the Quaker Colony was advancing its land prices and announcing:

"Whittier is the coming place! It will dwarf Monrovia and eclipse Pasadena. Nothing can stop it! The Quakers are coming from all over the United States."

The Quakers were coming! Late in the afternoon of July 18, 1887, the first carload of Quakers—from Iowa—reached Norwalk. The car was pushed onto a siding for the night. Next morning the colonists were greeted by Jonathan Bailey, who brought a box of apricots, and William P. Cooper, who brought a spring wagon. Thirteen Quakers climbed into the wagon and two girls mounted the ponies that Cooper led up to carry the overflow.

The wagon party turned northeast. Halfway to Whittier they stopped at Fulton Wells, now Santa Fe Springs, for a drink of sulphur water. On toward the hills they drove and presently reached the colony of their dreams.

They saw a partly finished store building at the southwest corner of Greenleaf Avenue and Philadelphia Street, a small structure at the northwest corner of Philadelphia Street and Milton Avenue (which Cooper said was his home), a large tent on the opposite corner (where the party was to eat), a black water tank and farther back an old ranch house surrounded by pepper trees.

Today

The Quaker Colony of 1887 is now a city of shaded streets, good homes and seventeen thousand people devoted to pleasant living and the production of oranges, avocados, oil, and college graduates. Whittier looks out over its miles of fruit trees and recalls that once all its water came from springs in Turnbull Canyon. It remembers its founders and the people—Quakers and non-Quakers—who have shaped it into a modern city. It remembers several depressions and several booms. Whittier looks out over the broad valley and, when it is reminiscent, sees Indian brush huts in the "place of wild bees," sees the vineyards of Manuel Nieto and the Spanish colonists, sees cattle and horsemen on El Camino

Real, sees Pico's hacienda and the chapel across the way, sees a flood and a river changing its course, and sees a road wide with the ruts of wagon wheels endlessly bringing in people from over the mesa.

When Andrés Pico Lived in San Fernando Mission

SAN FERNANDO VALLEY

and the story of the
RANCHO EX-MISSION DE SAN FERNANDO

IN AUGUST OF 1769 the first party of white men crossed the San Fernando Valley on their way north toward Monterey Bay. They were under the leadership of Portolá. Leaving the Los Angeles and Westwood area, they had turned north into the Santa Monica Mountains, following an Indian trail up Sepulveda Canyon.

It was hard going, according to Father Juan Crespi, whose diary of the trip has made him famous. At the crest the vast San Fernando plain stretched before them.

74

"We saw a very pleasant and spacious valley," Crespi wrote. "We descended to it and stopped close to the watering place, which is a very large pool. Near it we found a large village of heathen, very friendly and docile; they offered us their seeds in baskets and other things made of rushes. There were so many that if more of them had come with arms it would have caused us some suspicion, for we counted more than two hundred, men, women, and children. Each of them brought some food with which to regale us, and we reciprocated with beads and ribbons . . . We gave to this plain the name of Valley of Santa Catalina de Bononia de los Encinos. It is nearly three leagues wide and more than eight long. It has on its hills and in its valleys many live oaks and walnuts, though small. . . ."

*1769
Village
of Heathen*

That was on August 5, 1769. The camping place was in the present Encino area, probably near the reservoir that can be seen today from Ventura Boulevard in front of the Amestoy (formerly the Vicente de la Osa) ranch house. Here the ancient springs of water still gush forth and here the old Indian village site still yields its relics.

The next day was Sunday and "we rested," said Crespi, "receiving innumerable visits from heathen who came to see us from different parts . . ."

Monday the party crossed the San Fernando Valley.

"A little before three in the afternoon we set out to the north and crossed the plain, which is about three leagues wide, and went to camp at the foot of the mountains in a very green valley grown with large live oaks and alders . . ."

Five years later, in 1774, Juan Bautista de Anza, first to make the overland journey to California from Sonora by way of the Colorado Desert, traversed the length of the valley. He did it again in 1776 and in that same year Francisco Garcés, who had opened a California route via the Mojave River and Cajon Pass, entered the San Fernando area.

To walk in one day from San Gabriel Mission, founded in 1771, to that of San Buenaventura, founded in 1782, was too much even for a Franciscan friar. So, to help complete the chain of missions, an exploring party set out from San Buenaventura early in August of 1795 to find a site for a mission midway.

Seeking good land, abundant water and Indians, the missionary fathers finally chose as a proper place the upper end of the San Fernando Valley, or, as it was then called, the Encino (Oak) Valley.

*1795
Reyes
Rancho*

The spot chosen was the "Reyes Rancho," for it was being used by Francisco Reyes, alcalde of the pueblo of Los Angeles. It was "distant from the camino real about two leagues." Reyes had there a house, livestock and a field of corn, beans and melons, with Indians for ranch hands.

The Indian name for the place was *Achois Comihabit*.

"We found the place quite suitable for a mission," Father De Santa Maria had reported, "because it has much water, much humid land and also limestone; for we came upon a party of gentiles who were finishing a kiln for burning lime which they had already heaped up. Stone for the foundations of the buildings is nearby. There is pine timber in the direction of west-northwest of said locality, not very far away; also pastures are to be found and patches very suitable for cattle; but there is a lack of firewood; for the place has no more than is found in the arroyo, which is about one league long. There we found willows, poplars, alders, and a few live-oaks, at a distance of a quarter or a half league from the mission, if it should be founded there. In this place we came to a rancheria near the dwelling of said Reyes—with enough Indians."

The name "San Fernando Rey" was given to the proposed mission, after Ferdinand III of Spain.

The mission was founded on September 8, 1797. Father Lasuen was in charge of the ceremonies and to the Governor he reported:

1797
Mission
Founded

"In the presence of many pagans of both sexes and all ages, who manifested a good deal of pleasure and satisfaction, I blessed the water, the site, and a large cross, which we planted and venerated. I concluded the function by solemnly singing Te Deum . . . I then baptized those offered . . . Thus we took possession of the site by dedicating it in honor of the glorious San Fernando, King of Spain."

To help the new establishment other southern California missions sent cattle, horses, mules and sheep—nearly a thousand animals.

The crops were put in, to be irrigated by water from the nearby ciénegas or springs that for unnumbered years had drawn the Indians of the valley. A small dam was built. From the reservoir formed, clay pipes conveyed the water.

A temporary church and quarters for the priests and soldiers were put up, then granaries and storerooms, and later huts for the neophytes.

Meanwhile the converts and the cattle increased in number and the Mission's sway extended over the entire valley, including the areas long years later to be given over to the settlements and cities of Van Nuys, North Hollywood, Reseda, Sepulveda, Canoga Park, Chatsworth Park, Northridge, Pacoima, Sunland, Tujunga, Roscoe, Studio City, Granada, Sherman Oaks, Encino, Tarzana, Girard, Calabasas and San Fernando. Indians to be baptized came from nearly 200 different Indian rancherias, including Cahuenga, Camulos, Piru, Topanga, Simi and Tujunga.

While Mexico was revolting against Spain in 1821 life in the San Fernando Valley continued its pastoral way, centering about the Mission and prospering.

In 1822 there were 1001 Indian neophytes living at the Mission itself. Under the direction of the padres the men and boys were taught to farm the fields—set out to wheat, barley, corn, beans and peas—to plant and care for fruit trees, to raise cattle, horses and sheep, to

1822
Many
Neophytes

cure hides, tend vineyards and make wine, as well as to be carpenters, masons, tailors, and shoe-makers. Their activities had made the whole valley spring to life.

In that year the broad San Fernando plain supported 7000 cattle, 6500 sheep, 40 goats, 50 pigs, 1320 horses and 80 mules, all Mission-owned.

The pastoral way, however, was not made up entirely of sunshine, attendance at mass, joyous labor, horse-racing and fiestas. It is recorded that the workers in the fields had to contend with caterpillars, locusts, rabbits and worms, and that both Indian men and Indian women sometimes strayed from the narrow path laid down by the padres.

The movement to secularize California missions, long under way, reached San Fernando in October of 1834.

As at other missions, a superintendent, or major-domo, was placed in charge to manage the properties for the State.

1834 Seculariza-tion

San Fernando Rey suffered less from secularization than most missions. It continued to prosper for many seasons, though year by year the Indians drifted away and the flocks grew less.

Through Catalina Lopez, daughter of Don Pedro Lopez, major-domo, this picture of the period has come down:

". . . . San Fernando was widely famous for its fiestas, which were many, but the greatest of the year was on May 30th, San Fernando or Saint Ferdinando Day. People from all southern

California gathered at San Fernando on this day to taste the first fruits of the year. The day was begun by attending mass. All attended, from the major-domo to the lowliest Indian. Following the mass was a great feast or banquet. The table was spread between two long rows of pomegranate trees in the orchard at the rear of the old church. In the afternoon such sports as horse racing were enjoyed, but the main event was a bull fight held in the plaza in front of the old church. In the evening, songs and dancing ended the gay fiesta. The Indians had special fiestas, whole tribes making the yearly pilgrimage, coming from great distances. The feature of the fiesta was a dance in which all the members of the different tribes joined. A large image of the Indian chief was erected, around which a fire was built. As the dancers moved in the circle about the image they cast into the fire some personal belongings of their dead. The music to the dance was the wailing and weeping of the dancers themselves."

In December of 1836 Juan B. Alvarado took Monterey, the capital city of California, Governor Gutierrez surrendering. Alvarado represented current opposition of Californians to their Mexican officials. He marched south to take Los Angeles.

1837
Armed
Men

Los Angeles prepared to defend herself. For a war chest she took $2000 of the San Fernando Mission funds. Indians and rancheros were enlisted. By the middle of January in 1837 a force of nearly 300 men was established at San Fernando, ready to oppose Alvarado, his army and his two pieces of artillery.

Between Calabasas and Encino, Alvarado was met by Mayor Sepulveda of Los Angeles and Vicente de la Osa of Encino. For two days they talked.

All went well until Alvarado was asked to disband his army. That was too much. His reply was to send a messenger to San Fernando demanding immediate surrender, threatening to take it by force.

"San Fernando is at your disposal," was the message sent back to Alvarado.

Alvarado promptly occupied San Fernando and, a few days later, Los Angeles. With this the war ended, the soldiers disbanded and the differences were settled by agreement.

Francisco Lopez, brother of Don Pedro, was one day rounding up some stray horses in Placerita Canyon, north of the mission. He and his companion stopped to rest beneath a tree. While doing so, Lopez took his knife and dug up some wild onions.

Attached to the roots was a nugget of gold. Further digging showed other nuggets.

This happened on March 9, 1842, six years before Marshall's famous discovery at Sutter's Mill.

1842
Gold

Prospectors worked in Placerita Canyon for a number of years, taking out six to eight thousand dollars a year. Then the Placerita fever died out and the first discovery of gold came to nothing.

When the last Franciscan had left San Fernando and

when almost every vestige of the old life had passed away, the government leased the land to Andrés Pico and Juan Manso for a nine-year period. This was in 1845.

Juan Manso had been appointed as commissioner to make inventories of mission estates.

Pico was a better soldier than rancher, it is said. Although he remained in possession for a number of years, some of the buildings were allowed to fall into ruin, the orchards, fields and cattle to be neglected.

It was in this same year of 1845 that the famous battle of Cahuenga, or Alamo, was fought—famous because its only casualties were one horse killed and one mule wounded.

1845
Battle of
Cahuenga

Between Encino and Cahuenga Pass, on the afternoon of February 20th, Governor Micheltorena's forces exchanged cannon-shots with General Castro's rebelling Californians.

Non-combatants in Los Angeles assembled on a hilltop and prayed for the safety of their embattled relatives.

The next morning the long-distance conflict was resumed—on the Verdugo Ranch.

The armies were reluctant, and the Americans on both sides preferred fraternizing to fighting.

Micheltorena finally raised the white flag and the next day California had Pio Pico—the brother of Andrés —for its governor.

Ordinarily, a Mexican grant of a rancho was the gift of the government. But in the case of the San Fernando the government made a sale—to raise money in defense of California against the invading Americans.

The purchaser was Don Eulogio de Celis who paid $14,000 for 13 square leagues of land. On June 17, 1846, Governor Pico gave him a deed. *116 858 A*

In the transfer, the church and its appurtenances were reserved. Henceforth the property sold was called "Rancho Ex-Mission of San Fernando."

By the terms of the deed the new owner agreed to take care of the "old Indians" during their lifetime and to respect their right to plant crops. He also agreed to "warrant" to the Father Minister "subsistence and clothing with all possible decency together with the rooms assigned to him or those which he justly requires."

In later years when Pico was put on the witness stand and questioned by United States Land Commissioner Hall as to this transaction, he said:

> "I made the grant under and by virtue of my authority as governor and for the purpose of providing means to carry on the war . . . I had authority to make the grant by virtue of instructions from the Minister of War and Marine of Mexico."

At this point in his testimony Pico produced a paper from his pocket. It was a document dated March 10, 1846. It was from the Minister of War and Marine to the General Commander of the Californias. Pico read its contents:

> "The preparations which the United States

*1846
Eulogio
de Celis*

*1 + 7/10 cents
per acre*

are making and the approach of their naval forces leave no doubt that war is about to break out, and as His Excellency the President, pro tem, is resolved to sustain the rights of the Nation, he wishes that in all the ports of the Republic where the enemy may present himself a rigorous defense be made, capable of giving honor and glory to the National Flag. For that object and until the Supreme Government appropriates and sends you the necessary means he relies upon your patriotism and fidelity to dictate the measures which you may judge necessary for the defense of that Department, for which purpose you and His Excellency are invested with full powers. And I have the honor to insert the same to you for your cognizance, hoping that you on your part will lose no efforts to preserve the rights of the Nation."

Pico went on to tell that the purchase price of the ranch was thought to be a fair price and that it was applied to the defense of the country.

Eulogio de Celis, who bought the ranch, was a native of Spain, coming to California at least as early as 1836. In that year he was a supercargo in the employ of Henry Virmond, a merchant of Acapulco and and the City of Mexico who owned several vessels in the California trade. He made Los Angeles his home, the Celis house being across from the Bella Union Hotel on Main Street.

Four years after he bought San Fernando he was

listed in the Los Angeles County census (of 1850) as an agriculturist, 42 years old and the owner of real estate worth $20,000.00.

It has been mentioned that Celis, owner of the ranch, was an ex-employee of the trader Virmond. So was Juan Manso, who had leased the ranch, and so was Edward Vischer, later to be attorney in fact for Celis and to become well known as an artist.

American soldiers, under Fremont, entered San Fernando Valley January 11, 1847. They came through Fremont Pass and were met by Geronimo Lopez, a boy of sixteen, to welcome them to the Mission.

1847
Fremont's
Soldiers

Fremont rested at the Mission, he and Don Pedro Lopez becoming good friends. On the thirteenth he went on to Cahuenga to sign the treaty between the Americans and the Californians, the latter having yielded to the inevitable. Andrés Pico signed as commander of the Californians.

By the Treaty of Guadalupe Hidalgo, California was ceded to the United States in 1848. Two years later it was admitted as a state to the Union.

1848
Treaty

Eulogio de Celis filed his claim with the United States Board of Land Commissioners in October of 1852 to all the leagues of land deeded him by Pio Pico.

After investigation, and after calling in Nemicio Dominguez of Santa Barbara, who was an authority on the San Fernando Valley and its occupancy, Pio Pico, who gave the deed, and Augustin Olvera, who wrote the deed, the Board confirmed the claim, saying:

"The genuineness of the grant is clearly established, and the circumstances under which it was made so clearly explained as to leave no doubt but it was done in good faith."

The United States District Court upheld the Board's findings and on January 8, 1873, a patent was issued by the United States, the survey showing 116,858.43 acres.

The same Board confirmed the Church's title to the Mission and grounds immediately surrounding, amounting to 170.20 acres. On May 3, 1862, the United States issued its patent to Joseph S. Alemany, Roman Catholic Bishop of the Diocese of Monterey.

The Board also confirmed the valley grant of Rancho El Encino, which went to Vicente de la Osa (successor to the Indians, Ramon, Francisco and Roque). It was he who built the adobe house, still standing, used first by himself, then by Eugene Garnier and later by the Amestoy family. Another valley confirmation was of Rancho El Escorpion to Urbano, Odon and Manuel, Indians, and to Joaquin Romero.

In 1853 the first purchaser and owner of San Fernando left his vast rancho and returned to his native Spain.

Before leaving he appointed Edward Vischer his attorney in fact.

Celis never returned to California. He died in the city of Bilbao, Spain, on January 27, 1869, after which his widow and children came back to southern California. The eldest son, Eulogio F., was appointed administrator of his father's estate.

Andrés Pico, who had been in possession of the ranch since 1845, got a deed to a half interest in 1854 for $1854.00, through Edward Vischer, attorney in fact for Eulogio de Celis and his wife, Josefa Arguello de Celis.

He also got a year's lease, beginning January 1, 1855, of the "appurtenances," including 50 head of wild horses and mares, 37 head of cattle and 1 yoke of oxen. The rental was $1.00 a month.

1855
Lease to
Andrés Pico

Early in the sixties Geronimo Lopez and his wife, who was Catalina, Don Pedro's daughter, moved to a forty-acre tract near the Mission. The property they bought was part of land given many years before to a mission Indian named Samuel who had planted an orchard to oranges, pears and pomegranates, and had set out a vineyard.

Here they built a large adobe home which, like the Mission, became a landmark in the valley. It became known as Lopez Station, for Geronimo kept the stage-house. Here the twenty-mule teams of Remi Nadeau stopped overnight on their way from Los Angeles up to the Cerro Gordo Mines in Inyo County. Here the first postoffice was established, in 1869. In a house a little to the north the Lopez family started the first English-speaking school.

1869
Post-
Office

A curious map recorded in 1872 in Book 2, Pages 250 and 251 in the Miscellaneous Records of Los Angeles County, shows the location of these buildings and the old highway. Today part of the area is covered by reservoirs of the City of Los Angeles.

During the late Sixties and early Seventies a visitor riding horseback through the high wild mustard would have seen no evidence of human activity in the whole wide San Fernando Valley except the Mission, perhaps Lopez Station and a few other nearby adobes, and cattle grazing in fields.

Andrés Pico, on May 21, 1862, had conveyed all his interest in the San Fernando Rancho to his brother Pio, who in turn sold to the San Fernando Farm Homestead Association on July 2, 1869. Pio Pico's price was $115,000.00.

He held back certain specified areas including 1000 acres near the mission. Andrés continued to live in the central building of the mission, though the outer buildings were allowed to fall into ruin.

*1871
Lankershim
& Van Nuys*

The Association brought a friendly action for partition against the heirs of Eulogio de Celis. By decree of the District Court in 1871 it got full title to the southerly portion of the valley. This amounted to nearly 60,000 acres, including what in time was to become Van Nuys, North Hollywood, Reseda, Canoga Park and Encino.

Back of the Association were several San Francisco men, chief of whom was Isaac Lankershim, who had come south in 1869 and had been impressed by the height of the wild oats growing in San Fernando Valley.

Later Isaac Newton Van Nuys came into the valley and joined his friend Lankershim with whom he had been associated in the north.

Two drought years caused the death of 40,000 sheep.

Lankershim and Van Nuys decided then to go in for wheat-raising instead of sheep-raising.

The southerly half of the San Fernando Valley, under the guidance of Lankershim and Van Nuys, became a vast wheat ranch, with Liverpool, England, as one of its markets.

The corporate life of the Association was five years from June 22, 1869. On February 3, 1880, the trustees distributed the property to the stockholders, largest of whom was James B. Lankershim, son of the original Lankershim, who had been superintendent of the ranch for a number of years.

Senator Charles Maclay of Santa Clara wanted land in southern California. The upper portion of San Fernando Valley, which was then threatened with foreclosure, was recommended to him by his friend Governor Leland Stanford.

The Senator went to Los Angeles, hired a team and drove out through Cahuenga Pass.

As he looked down into the San Fernando Valley he is said to have exclaimed: "This is the Garden of Eden."

At any rate the Senator was satisfied. He went to Eulogio F. de Celis, who was the administrator of his father's estate, and in April of 1874 entered into a written agreement for the purchase of the 56,000-acre ranch which extended from the mountains back of Chatsworth on the west to the Roscoe area on the east. He had in mind its division into small tracts and then its sale and colonization.

During August and September he bought the ranch, with the help of a loan from his friend Stanford, and acquired a partner who was interested in farming.

The partner was George K. Porter, a San Francisco shoe manufacturer. Porter advanced $66,797.00 and Maclay $13,580.95 toward the purchase from the heirs of Eulogio de Celis. They assumed a $16,000 mortgage given by certain of the heirs, and Maclay, on his one-fourth interest, gave back a purchase price mortgage of $37,500.00. Buying the ranch involved clearing its title. They got deeds from Alfred A. Cohen who held a foreclosed portion, and from the holders of other adverse interests. They quieted title against others.

A few years later another Porter—Benjamin F. from Santa Cruz County—joined his cousin in ownership of the north half of the valley. In January of 1879 George K. Porter deeded him a half interest in his three-fourths. A few months later he succeeded to a part of Charles Maclay's fourth.

Under the direction of Maclay and the Porters the north half of the valley, like the south half, became a wheatfield.

Senator Maclay paid a visit to the County Recorder in Los Angeles on the afternoon of September 15, 1874.

He carried with him for recording a subdivision map showing streets, blocks and several thousand twen-

ty-five-foot lots—enough to take care of an army of land-buyers. It was labeled "Map of the City of San Fernando." *1874*
San
Fernando

The new town extended southwesterly from the Southern Pacific right of way, and partly encircled the "Pico Reserve." Adjoining the railroad were a depot, a hotel and the Cerro Gordo Freighting Company's property. The streets bore such well known southern California names as Nadeau, Celis, Pico, Coronel, Kewen, Griffith, Mott, O'Melveny, Widney, Sepulveda, Temple, Downey, Hellman, Banning, Requena, Beaudry, Wolfskill and Newmark.

In this year of the town's founding, excursion trains brought throngs of people from Los Angeles to look over the new town and have lunch at the Mission. Persons intending to become residents traveled half rate. Those who drove followed roads hub-deep with dust.

Town lots were offered at $10 to $25 each, farming lands at $5 to $40 an acre.

A small hotel, the Kittridge House, was built, and then another, the Fernando.

Seven saloons came to life.

Remi Nadeau, making the new town his headquarters, brought in 80 teamsters and 1600 mules, built barns and warehouses.

At Maclay's store the townspeople and the ranchers could get their supplies and have their checks cashed.

For himself and his family the Senator built a two-story Colonial home at the corner of Celis and Workman Streets.

Since the spring of 1875 fifteen hundred men, chiefly Chinese coolies, had been digging a tunnel through the mountains northwest of San Fernando. This was to link northern with southern California, by rail, and to put Los Angeles on the transcontinental line of the Southern Pacific that had already reached San Francisco a few years before.

1876
Railroad
Celebration

On September 5, 1876, a golden spike was driven to celebrate the completion of 6900 feet of tunnel. The ceremony was held near Lang Station, with the governor, railroad officials and prominent Californians—including Senator Maclay—in attendance, and with the Chinese laborers lined up on both sides of the track and presenting their shovels.

Henceforth the markets of San Francisco and the east would be open to Los Angeles' seven thousand inhabitants, to the people of San Fernando Valley and the rest of southern California. The period of growth would begin.

A new corporation, the Los Angeles Farm and Milling Company, had been organized in San Francisco to succeed to the San Fernando Farm Homestead Association. Its directors were practically the same. To it the stockholders of the dissolved corporation deeded the south half of the valley. This was on February 7, 1880.

The success of wheat-raising had led to flour-milling and, in the year 1888, 510,000 bushels of wheat were produced by the Los Angeles Farm and Milling Company.

Meanwhile, the upper half of the valley, controlled by Maclay and Porter, had become a giant field of waving wheat and barley.

Unable to agree on policies, the partners decided to divide the upper portion of the San Fernando Valley.

Senator Maclay, who wished to subdivide, took the portion northeast of the main line of the Southern Pacific Railroad and east of Pacoima Creek or Wash.

Letting the toss of a coin decide their fate, Benjamin F. Porter became sole owner of the lands west of Aliso Canyon and west of the present Zelzah Avenue, including the Chatsworth Park area, and George K. Porter the owner of the center portion.

Each of the three got approximately 20,000 acres.

Early in 1888 the Lankershim Ranch Land and Water Company bought from the Los Angeles Farm and Milling Company the east 12,000 acres of its land. This new corporation's first directors were L. T. Garnsey, F. C. Garbutt, S. W. Luitweiler, William Bogel, C. W. Smith and W. S. De Van.

1888-9 Boom

By May the 12,000 acres, whose west boundary today is Whitsett Avenue, had been subdivided into lots of various sizes, chiefly 40-acre parcels. The subdivision was placed on the market with prices ranging from $5 to $150 an acre.

Presently a town sprang up. It was called Toluca for a while, later Lankershim. Today it is North Hollywood.

This boom town of the Eighties had a general store —the "Weddington Bros."—supplying all the settlers in the south half of the valley. The store also served as a postoffice. There was a hotel, of course, a blacksmith shop and a school house.

In the north half of the valley George K. Porter in 1887 deeded a large portion of his acreage southwest of the town of San Fernando and the Mission to the newly organized Porter Land and Water Company, the directors of which were Dan McFarland, Jesse Yarnell, John B. Baskin, E. A. Forrester, L. T. Garnsey. George K. Porter held most of the stock. The deed, recorded in July of 1887, showed a consideration of $100,000.00. By January 10th following, a subdivision map had been prepared with the property cut up into 10-acre and 40-acre lots. Its boundary on the west was Balboa Boulevard, on the east Pacoima Creek and on the south Roscoe Boulevard.

An irrigation system was put in, to take care of 4000 acres. A street railway was built. One hundred and seventy acres of navel oranges were planted. A three-story hotel—the Mission—was erected to handle the tourists.

In the town of San Fernando a brick building arose at the corner of Maclay and Second Street. Another hotel, the Rey, came into existence, also the Buckhorn Stables. Many homes were built. Orange groves were set out.

Senator Maclay, not satisfied with giving the town of San Fernando its start, nor with all his valley activities including filling a Methodist pulpit and founding and endowing Maclay College of Theology, succumbed to the current subdivision fever. He organized a group of capitalists, with H. L. Macneil, George C. Hagar, J. K. Alexander, R. M. Widney and himself as its trustees. They took the portion northeast of San Fernando Road and east of Pacoima Creek—the 20,000-acre parcel allotted to Senator Maclay in the partition. With the help of an engineer named William P. Granger, they subdivided this enormous area into 40-acre farm lots, enough to take care of a vast army of colonists. The townsite of Pacoima was laid out also at this time and within this tract. It was located on the railroad southeast of San Fernando.

B. F. Porter did not go in so heavily for subdivisions as his former partners. He did sell, however, a large acreage on the west boundary of the ranch to the San Fernando Valley Improvement Co. This went into the subdivision known to this day as "Chatsworth Park," the map of which was recorded March 10, 1888.

In the late Eighties the people were coming into the valley that had once been under the control of Franciscan fathers.

Throughout the wheatfields of the San Fernando Valley—north and south, east and west—ranch homes, marked out fields, fruit trees, tiny clusters of buildings, the beginnings of communities—all were making their imprint on the land.

With a keen eye for its future possibilities, Leslie C. Brand, budding capitalist, took an option to buy the remaining holdings of the Porter Land and Water Company, amounting to 16,000 acres.

*1903
Brand's
Option*

He surrounded himself with such influential men as Henry E. Huntington, E. H. Harriman, Harrison Gray Otis, W. G. Kerckhoff, J. F. Sartori and E. T. Earl, and on December 1, 1904, organized the San Fernando Mission Land Company. The Company then took up Brand's option, paying $160,000.00 in cash and $390,000.00 in bonds of the new corporation for the property that had once been George K. Porter's.

John T. Wilson, ranch manager for the Porter Land and Water Company, became superintendent under the new owners. Wilson, living in the valley since boyhood, had married the daughter of Don Geronimo Lopez and had been active in all valley affairs.

The Pacific Electric Railway was brought to San Fernando, Brand Boulevard extended, the Porter Hotel built and the San Fernando National Bank organized.

Meanwhile the Los Angeles Aqueduct was under construction, destined to make San Fernando Valley land fertile and valuable and to be followed by the Valley's annexation to the City of Los Angeles.

Brand and his associates conducted a heavy selling campaign, re-subdivided part of their land, and between 1916 and 1923 orchards, cultivated fields and the homes of new owners made a wide pattern of activity.

The land directly opposite the Mission was given the City of Los Angeles. Brand Park, gay with its plantings and flowers, today looks upon the buff Mission walls across the street, adding to the charm of one of California's most attractive scenes.

The completion of the Los Angeles Aqueduct—one of the greatest of modern engineering tasks—brought the water of the high Sierras to San Fernando.

On the fifth of November, 1913, the people assembled at the San Fernando Reservoir saw mountain waters from 250 miles away come plunging down the open aqueduct—the end of a job started in 1908 by engineer William Mulholland, the beginning of a new day not only for Los Angeles but for a great valley.

1913 Aqueduct

Since the aqueduct would not come to Los Angeles, Los Angeles went to the aqueduct.

On May 22, 1915, the greater portion of the San Fernando Valley—nearly 170 square miles—was annexed to Los Angeles.

Owensmouth, now Canoga Park, came into the City in 1917, West Lankershim in 1919, Chatsworth in 1920, Lankershim in 1923.

San Fernando, incorporated in 1911, has retained its identity, though surrounded on all sides by the City of Los Angeles. END FINIS

The explorer of 1939 may enter the San Fernando Valley by almost the same route that Portolá took in 1769. He will follow a broad, paved highway—Sepulveda Boulevard—today's transformation of the Indian trail that once led through Sepulveda Canyon.

1939 Exploring the Valley

Sepulveda Boulevard takes the modern traveler into the valley and to the beginning of a trip that will carry him through a series of suburban settlements, active towns, a continuous "population area" of green, tree-lined fields, fruit orchards, small farms, ample estates and shining white and buff homes.

Near where Sepulveda crosses Ventura Boulevard is *SHERMAN OAKS*, which the billboards describe as a "1000-acre community development." Here the wider canyons of the Santa Monicas permit hillside estates and lowland homes set among crouching oaks.

Continuing west on Ventura Boulevard, the road follows approximately the route of the Anza party of 1774.

Just before reaching *ENCINO*, today's explorer sees on his right the adobe home that was once Vicente de la Osa's and the shining water coming from springs that satisfied the thirst of Portolá's men. At Encino the hillsides are patterned with charming dwellings. Rich grasses sweep down over the scene. Many motion picture people, including Al Jolson, Ruby Keeler, Edward Everett Horton and the Spencer Tracys, are among its citizens.

On through *TARZANA*, the home of Edgar Rice Burroughs, and through *GIRARD*, where, in both communities, curving hills come down to the boulevard and tall eucalyptus trees edge grassy fields.

At *CALABASAS* the valley begins to lose itself in the boundary hills. Where a sign says "Los Angeles City Limits," a tiny community has centered for many years about several giant oaks. A few old dwellings suggest the pastoral days, and stories may be picked up out of the past of violence among sheep herders and of hanging "bees." Here the Franciscan exploring party spent a night on the trip to pick a mission site. Not far away are private horse and cattle ranches and the estates of Clarence Brown, who succeeded to King C. Gillette's property, and of Joel McCrea and Frances Dee.

Retracing Ventura Boulevard and turning north just east of Girard the tourist comes into the community of *CANOGA PARK* (formerly Owensmouth), located on flat, fertile acres devoted to alfalfa, sugar beets and grain. A well groomed business district centers at Sherman Way and Canoga Avenue, upon which 12,000 people depend. The writers Florence Ryerson and Colin Clements, in their "Shadow Ranch" on Vanowen Street, have one of the most interesting ranch houses and some of the tallest eucalyptus trees in the valley. They keep close to the community center, unlike rancheros Joe E. Brown and Francis Lederer, whose places are far off to the northwest.

Continuing east on Sherman Way, through alfalfa fields the traveler comes into *RESEDA*, another attractive center of activity that—like Canoga Park—is destined for quick growth. It is an area of both large and small ranches, producing good crops of walnuts, fruits, berries, lettuce and lima beans.

Going north on Reseda Boulevard one passes through an older farming settlement, first known as Zelzah and later as North Los Angeles. The more distinctive title of *NORTHRIDGE* has just been adopted by its people, who now begin to benefit from the flood of newcomers to the valley.

Continuing north the tour carries one into the shining area of the B. F. Porter Estate lands, the "Northridge District." Ten thousand rolling acres, commanding a magnificent view of green fields and blue distant hills, have been broken into large ranch estates. "Marwyck," owned by Barbara Stanwyck and Marion (Mrs. Zeppo) Marx, occupies 140 acres. West on Devonshire is the orange grove and home of Richard Arlen. Then "Kellymac" looms up, the setting for the residence and guest house of Paul Kelly, pioneer among the actors who have taken the Northridge District to heart. On one side of Kelly is Carole Lombard's place and on the other the 27-acre estate of Robert Taylor. Here in the Northridge District early California ranch houses and English homes occupy knolls that look down upon alfalfa and barley fields, fenced paddocks, badminton courts, stables, training tracks, polo ponies and swimming pools.

West of this district and beneath the shoulder of the boundary mountains is *CHATSWORTH PARK*, dating from the boom of the Eighties. Centering at Devonshire and Topanga Canyon Boulevard, Chatsworth Park has citrus groves, nurseries, small farms and fruit ranches, and draws motion picture companies to its superb setting.

Back on Devonshire Street and North on Zelzah Avenue the explorer of 1939 passes through the attractive citrus and small-ranch area of *GRANADA* and then drives into San Fernando.

SAN FERNANDO, the first city of the valley, has

maintained throughout the years its own identity and individuality. It has a population of 9500 and a business district that draws another 35,000. It is a large orange and lemon area, and close by is *SYLMAR*, famous for its olives since the early Nineties when the Los Angeles Olive Growers Association bought 1000 acres from the Maclay Rancho trustees.

1939
San
Fernando

San Fernando, active city though it is and on the main highway to the San Joaquin Valley, still has the flavor of its early days. Its visitors find that the old Mission, more beautiful in age than in youth, dominates the scene as it has ever since 1797. New enthusiasm is being put into its restoration.

Not only the Mission but some of San Fernando's homes carry the spirit of pastoral California days, especially the fine old adobe whose white walls can be glimpsed through the trees near the Mission, remodeled and preserved by its owner, M. R. Harrington.

Leaving San Fernando and its memories of Franciscan days, the tour continues into the well settled home and ranch region of *SEPULVEDA* in the heart of the Valley; then northward again toward San Fernando Road and into the broad plain upon which rises the town of *PACOIMA*, named after the canyon of the nearby mountains, and dating from the Eighties; and past gravel pits and rock crushers to *ROSCOE* at the Easterly boundary line of the Rancho Ex-Mission of San Fernando. At Roscoe 6000 people have poultry farms and in the more fertile areas, near the Verdugo Mountains, truck gardens and orange groves.

The tour turns now to *VAN NUYS* and *NORTH HOLLYWOOD*, active business, industrial, motion picture and residential communities that have risen on the great wheat ranches of the former owners. Van Nuys Boulevard is the backbone of Van Nuys and Lankershim Boulevard of North Hollywood. In the center of Van Nuys is the handsome Valley Municipal Building, administrative center of all the Los Angeles area of the valley. Both areas show vast activity in small-home construction, the level acres being patterned with the white and buff cubes of new houses. Close to Hollywood, they have the largest population of the valley.

STUDIO CITY and *UNIVERSAL CITY*, with their studios and gleaming business buildings, a visit to "Campo de Cahuenga," where the Treaty between Mexico and the United States was signed, and then to Ventura Boulevard. By Cahuenga Pass the explorer of 1939 leaves the San Fernando Valley.

Indian Village on La Ballona Creek

CULVER CITY

and the story of
RANCHO LA BALLONA and
RANCHO RINCON DE LOS BUEYES

THE CULVER CITY AREA was off the main highway of travel during the period of first white occupation of California which began in 1769.

It lay in the valley formed by La Ballona Creek flowing toward Playa del Rey, a year-round river draining the whole of the west Los Angeles region and fed directly from the chain of ciénegas and lakes that stretched from the Hollywood mountains to the Baldwin Hills. This valley was a place of rich silt, the higher ground being the present Culver City, the lower ground being the extensive marshes that stretch far back of the lagoon at La Ballona's mouth. Sycamores, willows and tules lined the river.

On old maps the cliffs of Ballona's easterly boundary are labeled "Gaucho," sometimes "Huacho," an Indian term meaning high place, according to Cristobal Machado of Culver City, whose memory of La Ballona Valley goes back to Indian days. It was against these cliffs that the Indians built their brush-and-mud huts. From them the brown-skinned men went forth to gather clams and shell fish at the beach beyond the lagoon, to hunt small game in the marshes and to find edible berries, seeds and insects in the river growth and on hillside shrubs.

Within the decade after the eleven families from Sonora and Sinaloa started building Los Angeles' first houses, the names of Machado, Higuera, Talamantes and Lopez were established in the community.

Members of these families were to become the first white settlers along Ballona Creek, the first white occupants of the valley land that stretches from Culver City to the sea.

One of the soldier-guard who came from Sonora to Los Angeles in 1781 was 25-year-old José Manuel Machado. He brought with him a 17-year-old wife, Maria. It was this Machado whose sons Augustin and Ygnacio were to settle Rancho La Ballona.

A few years after the founding of the pueblo, Felipe

Talamantes and his brother Tomas became Los Angeles citizens. Later they shared with the young Machado men in their ranch venture.

The alcalde of the pueblo in the year 1800 was Joaquin Higuera. His son, Bernardo, was to settle the land that adjoined the Rancho La Ballona on the northeast—Rancho Rincon de los Bueyes.

Meanwhile the people of the pueblo, with vague ideas about the boundaries of their own four square leagues of land, needed more good pasturage for their cattle. The Rincon and the Ballona, lying to the southwest, could qualify and in addition were so far from San Gabriel and San Fernando as to be unclaimed by the Missions.

At a very early period, then, cattle owners from the pueblo were visiting the Culver City valley.

"We occupied, with our grazing stock, houses and other interests, the place called 'Pass of the Carretas,' but more generally known by the name of the Ballona."

*1819-21
White
Settlers*

This was the statement of Augustin and Ygnacio Machado and Felipe and Tomas Talamantes. They made this statement on September 19, 1839, in a petition for confirmation of their title. It had been "about the space of eighteen or nineteen years," they said, "since they had moved in," under a permit from the military commander José de la Guerra y Noriega. Another source, the historian Bancroft, indicates the date was probably 1819, for in that year the Church was protesting, without avail, a cattle-grazing permit given by

Noriega to these four citizens of Los Angeles. The permit itself, unfortunately, is not among the United States Land Commission records, though it is referred to.

Augustin and Ygnacio Machado were young men in 1819—so young they would have received no ranch favors from the government, according to family tradition, without taking the older Talamantes brothers into partnership.

The road through the "Pass of the Carretas"—Paso de las Carretas it appears on first maps—was the ancestor of Washington Boulevard. To appreciate that this old sandy road was actually a pass between hills, the visitor of today need only stand on California Country Club or Pacific Military Academy property, and look toward the nearest point of the Baldwin Hills.

The Rincon was settled in the last month of 1821, under another concession from Noriega. A petition was delivered to him, written and dated on December 5, 1821. It read:

"To the Snr. Capn.

1821
A Petition
to Noriega

Bernardo Higuera and Cornelio Lopez, citizens of the Pueblo de Nuestra Señora la Reina de Los Angeles, and under the command of your honor, with the greatest respect and submission before your Excellency, appear and say that, possessing at the present time a number of cattle and not having any place so as properly to be able to keep them with a grazing ground of sufficient extent for the tithes required by our mother, the Holy Church—Therefore ask and beseech your extreme clemency to be pleased to grant to them the tract within this vicinity called *Corral Viejo del Rincon* so as that they may be able to place a corral for herding the said cattle unless it does some injury to the neighboring residents—a favor they expect from your extreme goodness and for which they will recognize themselves very grateful. May God preserve you many years."

This petition was signed at Los Angeles by Bernardo Higuera and Cornelio Lopez.

Two days later Noriega made an entry on the margin of the petition:

"Pueblo de Nuestra Señora de Los Angeles. Dec. 7, 1821. It is granted if no prejudice result to the community. (Signed) Noriega."

The origin of the word "Ballona" is in doubt. It does not appear on first maps. There is no basis in the old records or in local tradition for the common explanation of its being a corruption of "Ballena," meaning whale. "More likely," says Cristobal Machado, "it comes, somehow, from the word 'bay'." Certainly the bay was the big feature of Rancho La Ballona, for at flood time waters of the lagoon and the marshes backed up nearly to the present Culver City. Machado's explanation is borne out, too, in a story told many years ago by the Talamantes family to A. G. Rivera, Los Angeles County interpreter. Ballona, they said, was the California spelling of "Bayona," a bay city on the north coast of Spain from which one of their ancestors came.

The origin of "Rincon de los Bueyes"—corner for cattle—is simpler. The "Rincon," meaning corner, was the natural corral created by a ravine in the Baldwin Hills which lies just southwesterly of the large advertising sign of "57." From that "corner," with its rising knolls—attractive to grazing cattle—the name was applied to the rancho.

Shortly after Higuera and Lopez moved into the Rincon, Spanish control of California ended. Henceforth California was Mexican.

During the twenty years before 1839, when the title to La Ballona was confirmed, members of the Machado and Talamantes families, or their representatives, stocked the ranch with "large cattle and horses and small cattle" and improved it "with vineyards and houses and sowing grounds."

Augustin Machado married Ramona, the daughter of Francisco Sepulveda, a neighbor rancher. Augustin had built an adobe home near Ballona Creek, just northeast of the present Overland Avenue. One home, probably not his first, was washed away by floods. The next he placed on higher ground, in the same general location, but facing what is now Jefferson Boulevard. The site of the last ranch house is today a Japanese beetfield.

Ygnacio Machado married Estefana Palomares and had built a home farther up the stream.

The work of the ranch was done by the local Indians, one group of whom had their huts among the sycamores not far from Augustin's home, another group having their village against the hills beneath the present-day Loyola University.

Both brothers were widely known. They were respected as honorable men, generous and just.

On November 27, 1839, Governor Alvarado confirmed the Machado-Talamantes title by giving the four owners a grant. This followed the request made in September when they expressed a wish "to secure in the best possible mode the maintenance of our increased families." None of the four petitioners could write.

1839
From the
Governor

About a month later they were given formal, or "judicial," possession. This was done in the presence of the neighbors: Policarpio Higuera (of the Rancho Rincon de los Bueyes), who, incidentally, was one of the official cord-bearers at the ceremony; Antonio Ygnacio Avila (of Rancho Sausal Redondo); Francisco Sepulveda (of Rancho San Vicente); and Maximo Alanis (of Rancho San José de Buenos Ayres).

In 1833 or 1834 Ygnacio Machado had moved into the Cañada del Centinela, west of Inglewood's Centinela Springs. This left Augustin in full charge of La Ballona, for the Talamantes brothers lived on the Rincon de los Bueyes.

It was during this period and in the years following that Augustin Machado's white wine, produced on La Ballona, attained fame throughout California for its excellence. It ranked with the red wine for which San Gabriel was famous. Augustin's blond vintage cost ten dollars at the ranch for an eighteen-gallon barrel, and the agents sold it in the north for twenty-five dollars.

To get the necessities and luxuries that came only from New England and the Orient, it was Augustin's custom to go to San Pedro where the foreign traders anchored. He would send an ox-drawn carreta over the old road through the hills and over the site of Inglewood. He followed on horseback. One time, after selecting goods aboard ship, he was asked by the supercargo's new assistant to give a note or a guaranty—an unheard of procedure in California. For a moment Augustin was speechless. Then he pulled a hair from his beard, handed it to the youth and said: "Here, deliver this to Señor Aguirre (the ship owner). Tell him it is a hair from the beard of Augustin Machado."

Meanwhile there had been changes on the Rincon, where the Higueras went in for cattle, horses, corn, pumpkins and beans, as well as vineyards.

"It (the Rincon) was occupied when I first knew it," testified Januario Avila many years later, "by Bernardo Higuera jointly with Cornelio Lopez. Cornelio Lopez abandoned it and it was then occupied by Bernardo Higuera during his lifetime and after his death by his children. It is now (in 1852) occupied by Francisco Higuera, one of the sons of the late Bernardo. Bernardo built the two houses on the land about the year 1822 or 1823 and he lived on the land and the family have lived there ever since . . ."

Bernardo "verbally ceded" his interest to his brother Policarpio in 1834, according to the old records.

Policarpio, together with another brother, Mariano, Bernardo's son Francisco, and Pedro Mendez claimed title in 1848 by "denouncement," saying that the deceased Bernardo had abandoned the ranch. The 1836 census showed Bernardo and his wife, Maria Rosalia Palomares, living in Los Angeles.

1848
They
Denounce

"I lived in the family of the late Policarpio," said Francisco Botiller. "I also knew a man by the name of Pedro Mendez who lived on the rancho with Policarpio . . . I left the family quite young, but lived in their vicinity afterwards. I know when Mendez came there but cannot tell how long ago. I know when Mendez left, but cannot fix the time. It was after Policarpio's death, which happened soon after Micheltorena came to Los Angeles. After Policarpio's death, Mendez sold the small house he had on the place to Policarpio's widow for three or four tame cows, I believe, which were then worth about six dollars each. I was not present at the bargain, but I was told of it by both the widow and Mendez. I saw two of the cows in the possession of Mendez. Mendez then took away everything he had from the place and never returned . . ."

In 1843 Francisco Higuera was having a dispute with his fiery neighbor, Vicente Sanchez, who allowed hogs to pasture on the Rincon and who, Francisco feared, was claiming his land.

Francisco's adobe stood on the present site of the Casserini ranch house. It was close to La Ballona Creek, a clear stream with fine sandy bottom, where Francisco's nine children liked to swim. Not far from the adobe was the "little orchard," with its olive, apple, pear and pomegranate trees.

Francisco Higuera, it is told, fought in the Battle of San Pasqual—one of the sad preliminaries to the taking of California by the United States. He wounded and unhorsed Captain Gillespie and took Gillespie's saddle. "It was that fine saddle," Ynezita Higuera—Francisco's granddaughter—tells us, "that saved Gillespie's life."

1846 War

In October of 1852, two years after California came into the Union, the families owning La Ballona and El Rincon filed their claims with the United States Land Commission which had been established to settle all land claims.

The Machados and Talamantes had smooth sailing. The Board gave them its approval on February 14, 1854, and the United States District Court upheld the decision on appeal.

The Higueras were not so lucky. They were turned down at first. Not until the end of 1869 was their claim upheld in the District Court.

When the United States finally issued its patent covering Rancho La Ballona, on December 8, 1873, it confirmed the title to nearly 14,000 acres. The patentees were the original four claimants. The patent covering Rancho Rincon de los Bueyes, issued on August 27, 1872, confirmed title to 3100 acres, the patentees being Francisco and Secundino Higuera.

During the prosperous Fifties, when cattle products were in high demand, one Californian at least did not share in the prosperity.

Tomas Talamantes, one of the four owners of La Ballona, needed money. Two Americans, Benjamin D. Wilson—Don Benito he was called—and William T. B. Sanford, obliged him with a loan of $1500.

The note was dated June 14, 1854. It was to run for six months, with interest at five per cent per month until paid. The mortgage securing it covered Tomas' undivided fourth part of the whole rancho.

1854
A
Mortgage

Tomas was like other Spanish Californians who borrowed money from Yankee invaders. He couldn't keep up the interest. Before the end of the year the lenders had gone to court and recovered a judgment against him of $2353.26, with interest at five per cent per month from September 25, 1854, and an additional sum of $239.81. On December 6, 1855, a writ of execution was issued, and at that time the interest was $1690.28.

In the forenoon of December 31, 1855, a public auction sale by Sheriff Alexander was held in front of the court house in Los Angeles. Notice had been given in English and Spanish. The highest bidder was Benjamin D. Wilson whose offer was $2000.00.

On January 2, 1857, the Sheriff gave Wilson a deed, and Wilson became a fourth owner of a great rancho.

The death, the year before, of Felipe Talamantes—the oldest of the four original owners—helped further to complicate ranch ownership, for he left twenty-five heirs and devisees.

At the outset of the Civil War southern California's sympathies were so strongly southern that the national government kept it under close watch—with a force of troops established at Camp Latham on the slope of the Baldwin Hills near Ballona Creek.

The best known of the original four owners of La Ballona, Augustin Machado, died on May 17, 1865.

Augustin's wife was a Sepulveda, and Judge Sepulveda heard probate cases in Los Angeles County. So, the administration of the estate was transferred to San Bernardino County.

Two years later Ygnacio Machado deeded most of his interest in the ranch to relatives.

Partition of the Ballona was now unavoidable.

In 1859 Benjamin D. Wilson, the first American to be an owner of Rancho La Ballona, had sold his undivided fourth interest for $5500.00. The purchasers were John Sanford, James T. Young and John D. Young, who, in 1863, petitioned the District Court (Case 965) for a partition of the great ranch.

It took five years to obtain a partition decree.

In the partition of May 14, 1868, those who received allotments were:

John D. Young	Jesus Talamantes
George A. Sanford	Lauriano Talamantes
Elenda Young	Manuel Valenzuela
Addison Rose	Francisco Machado
Willis G. Prather	Dolores Machado
Macedonio Aguilar	Andrés Machado
Benina Talamantes	José Machado

Estate of Augustin Machado	Antonio Machado
Gregoria Talamantes	Rafael Machado
Tomasa Talamantes	Cristoval Machado
Pedro Talamantes	Ygnacio Machado
Jacinto Talamantes	

Each person got, in the partition, three kinds of land: "pasture" lands; "irrigable" lands; and "lands in Bay."

1868
Partition

Each person got beach frontage. To make this possible, it was necessary, in some instances, to describe and plat narrow strips of land connecting interior allotments with the sea. Some strips were two and a half miles long, though no wider than a city lot.

The largest allotments were to the "Estate of Augustin Machado." By a later partition, in 1875, these were redivided among the heirs of Augustin.

Upon the pasture lands allotted to Macedonio Aguilar was to arise most of Palms and later Culver City.

Will Tell, sometimes called William Tell, who once kept a paint shop in the Temple Block, Los Angeles, filed a preemption claim to one hundred and fifty acres in the vicinity of Del Rey Lagoon at the mouth of Ballona Creek.

On the edge of the lagoon he built a home for himself and Mrs. Tell. He called it Will Tell's Sea Shore Retreat, also Tell's Lookout. The lagoon became the William Tell Lake. The Tells got eight or ten boats, together with a supply of fishing tackle, guns and Don Mateo Keller's brandies. They ran the place for the benefit of picnic, boating and duck-hunting parties.

1871
A
Squatter

The widow of Augustin Machado started an action to evict the Tells in 1874, but it was allowed to lapse, and the Tells moved on to Santa Monica. An Irishman named Michael Duffy "took over" for a while, with his Hunter's Cottage, from which he advertised that he was prepared to "furnish sportsmen with board and lodging for man and beast." High tides came along, finally, to destroy the resort.

The whole marsh area of La Ballona long remained a favorite place for duck hunters. Among the gun clubs of the area were the Centinela, the Del Rey and the Recreation.

1886
The
Palms

Three subdividers, Joseph Curtis, E. H. Sweetser and C. J. Harrison, looked upon the good earth and the good location of Rancho La Ballona. They may have foreseen the boom that was about to hit southern California. These men laid out and subdivided a triangular tract, the map of which became official by its recording on December 24, 1886. They called it "The Palms."

The land within "The Palms" was bounded by Ballona Road, now Washington Boulevard, by First Street, now Overland Avenue, and by Manning Avenue.

The subdivision was carved out of a five hundred-acre tract which was a part of the Macedonio Aguilar allotment. Curtis, Sweetser and Harrison paid $40,000 for the five hundred acres. (Rita Botiller de Aguilar, widow of Macedonio, had succeeded to her husband's title in 1871. In 1883 she made a gift of the land to J. F. Figueroa, her grandson. Figueroa, six months later, sold the property to E. H. Owen and Albert Rimpau for

$17,500.00. He reserved for his own use seventeen acres, at the present northeast corner of Washington and Overland. In 1886 the new owners conveyed to W. A. Clinton, H. Clay Graham, J. M. Taylor and C. J. Fox, the sales price, still rising, being $37,500.00. A few months later the subdividers bought them out.)

Before this invasion of subdividers there were only two roads through the region—the one that is Washington and the other that forked off toward San Vicente (Santa Monica). For travelers there was the Half Way House, directly west of Francisco Higuera's adobe and half way between Los Angeles and Santa Monica—on the site of the Beacon Laundry near the Helms Bakeries. This House was well known for its wines and pickled olives.

The old ranchos of the Machado, Talamantes and Higuera families felt new stirrings of life when the real estate boom of the Eighties began to transform the landscape of southern California.

In "The Palms" the subdividers resubdivided, putting in more streets and more lots. In the Rincon de los Bueyes an old survey was brought out and recorded by José de Arnaz, who had bought a large portion northwest of Washington Boulevard from Secundino Higuera (in 1849) and Francisco Higuera (in 1867).

The greatest activity was at the mouth of La Ballona Creek, now Playa Del Rey, where a harbor—magnificently outlined on paper—was being constructed out of the old lagoon that had been the haunt of duck-hunters and picnickers since Indian days. The harbor was the brain child of Moye L. Wicks. He had been urging it since 1885, ever since Los Angeles began hunting for a tidewater terminal for the Santa Fe Railroad. The Ballona Harbor and Improvement Company, under the guidance of M. L. Wicks, H. W. Mills, R. F. Lotspeich, Frank Sabichi and others, was organized in 1886, with a capital stock of $300,000.00. Engineer Hugh Crable was employed to lay out a harbor to "float the fleets of the world."

By dredging, the Company hoped to create a 200-foot channel and an inner harbor two miles long, 300 to 600 feet wide and six to twenty feet deep. A right of way was granted the California Central Railway Company (Santa Fe) and a railroad was laid, connecting Los Angeles with the proposed harbor. A small steam dredger began work and two piers were constructed.

*1887
Port
Ballona*

Meanwhile, on the cliffs above, the "Town of Port Ballona" was laid out. The building of homes began and the sound of carpenters' hammers filled the air.

On August 21, 1887, the railroad was finished and the first train brought an excursion load of three hundred prominent Angelenos to Port Ballona. They listened to optimistic speeches and happy predictions.

The boom burst in 1888, the funds of the Ballona Harbor and Improvement Company became exhausted, the sands and the tides continued their opposition—and the dream of Port Ballona remained a dream.

Port Ballona, forgotten by all but antiquarians, was refurbished in 1902, given the euphonious name of Playa Del Rey and placed on the real estate market once more. Within Playa Del Rey's boundaries was included also the beach and land around the lagoon, all nicely subdivided and adorned with a long board walk.

This was in the beginning of the period of beach-town expansion in southern California, with the electric railroads behind the movement.

The subdivider was The Beach Land Company, Henry P. Barbour, president. Associated with Barbour were F. H. Rindge, M. H. Sherman, E. P. Clark, E. T. Earl, R. C. Gillis, Arthur Fleming, A. I. Smith and P. M. Green. This Company had acquired from Louis and Joseph Mesmer nearly all of the Town of Port Ballona and adjoining property. It gave a sixty-foot right of way to The Los Angeles-Hermosa Beach & Redondo Railway Company, succeeded by Los Angeles Pacific Company, which, in 1911, was to consolidate with the Pacific Electric Railway Company.

A new building period began. A pavilion costing $100,000.00 was built. An eighteen-mile speedway for automobile racing was constructed. The Hotel Del Rey, with fifty guest rooms, arose at a cost of $200,-000.00. The lagoon blossomed out with boathouse and grandstands. An inclined railway with two cars—"Alphonse" and "Gaston"—carried passengers up to an observation platform on the palisades above.

1902 Playa del Rey

Playa Del Rey was on all the excursion routes, and when the electric railroad established its famous "Balloon Trip" for the tourists, Playa Del Rey was a favorite stop. A fish dinner was served in the pavilion. The tourists were given time to look at the cliffs, the beach, and the lagoon with its "longest bridge span of reinforced concrete in the world," before being carried on to gather moonstones on Moonstone Beach near Redondo. Many bought lots and built attractive seaside homes along the beach in front of Rancho La Ballona.

For many years afterward Playa Del Rey was a popular seaside resort. On holidays it was crowded with auto-racing and boat-racing fans. But when the pavilion and hotel burned down, when the grandstand was removed and when sand filled the boat course, Playa Del Rey fell into decay.

Not until the middle twenties did subdividers come back and this time they devoted themselves successfully to the mesa and cliffs above.

Out of their efforts came "Palisades Del Rey" and "Surfridge"—residence areas still in the building—whose substantial homes command today a high view of the sea. At the foot of the cliffs is the attractive Westport Beach Club.

On July 16, 1912, the Washington Boulevard Improvement Company subdivided the remainder of Macedonio Aguilar's pasture-land.

1912 Washington Park

This was the 150-acre piece of land adjoining "The Palms" on the southeast that Macedonio Aguilar's grandson, J. F. Figueroa, sold to Victor Ponet in 1886 for $7500.00. It extended from Washington Boulevard to Ballona Creek and included much of the present Culver City. On the southwest it extended half a block beyond Jackson Avenue. It was officially named "Tract

No. 1775" but popularly called Washington Park. It carried the lay-out of streets, blocks and lots that has continued to date. Streets were given the names of presidents and other prominent figures in American history. Putnam Avenue was later to be changed to Culver Boulevard.

The Washington Boulevard Improvement Company did not buy this land directly from Victor Ponet. Ponet deeded to Alice Dana in 1906. Later in the same year Dana conveyed to M. J. Nolan, J. W. Vaughn and A. H. Busch, the three gentlemen whose title was acquired in 1912 by the subdividing corporation.

C. Cereghino guided this corporation. He and his associates from San Francisco and Oakland, on a trip through La Ballona, had picked this high land as the best for investment and subdivision. Cereghino is still satisfied with his selection for he lives today surrounded by orchard and garden on the acreage he reserved for himself on Madison Avenue, Culver City, within Tract No. 1775.

The announcement that a city, partly residential, partly business, was about to be born, climaxed a banquet held at the California Club in Los Angeles on July 25, 1913. At the tables sat the directors and stockholders of the newly formed Culver Investment Company, and a few of their friends. On this occasion the unborn town was christened "Culver City," honoring its enthusiastic father, Harry H. Culver.

1913 Christening a City

Culver, whose birthplace was Milford, Nebraska, and who had been educated in Nebraska, had come to

Los Angeles in 1910. He had gone into the real estate business, turning his attention to the land lying midway between Los Angeles and Venice.

Into the quiescent barley-field region of Palms, Washington Park and the surrounding countryside, where land was not "moving" fast enough to suit him, Harry Culver introduced new ideas in financing, advertising, and selling. He conceived the notion of a city on the highway between Los Angeles and the sea. He sought the help of the Pacific Electric Railway Company and of several land owners. He organized the Culver Investment Company, bought a group of blocks in Palms and some acreage adjoining: property lying northwest of Washington Boulevard. He secured the aid of P. H. Albright, civil engineer, and went to work on a subdivision that would form the heart of the city to be.

Bulletins issued from the Los Angeles offices of Harry H. Culver & Co., following the banquet at the California Club, throw sidelights on what was happening in the newly acquired barley fields and in lands in the area: —

July 27th—"Acreage values between Los Angeles and Venice are certain to experience a sharp advance."

August 17th—"Watch Los Angeles-Venice acreage go to $5000.00 . . . Culver City big improvement—work will begin . . . We have a few very attractive snaps."

August 31st—"The dirt is now flying fast.

Acreage values increasing with wonderful rapidity."

September 7th—"Intense activity. There are now thirty subdivisions. Venice is growing toward Los Angeles. Los Angeles is growing toward Venice."

On September 11, 1913, the Culver Investment Company's subdivision (Tract No. 2444) became official by being recorded in the County Recorder's office.

In later years, a local newspaper, in reminiscent mood, was able to say that "the fields became transformed and in their stead homes began to sprout and groups of industries and marts were springing up where barley leaves waved gently in the breeze."

Culver City, born in a whirl of real estate activity, was to become the community, "partly residential, partly business," that its founder planned.

The first building in the new subdivision was Harry Culver's real estate office. Before a year had gone by, there was a grocery store, a plumbing and hardware shop, a candy store, a newspaper (The Culver City Call), two churches, seven miles of sidewalks and curbs, a lighting system, a railroad station, an express company, a macaroni factory, many homes and 150 real estate salesmen.

Thomas H. Ince, producing pictures at Inceville, on the coast above Santa Monica, needed a stream of water that could float three canoes full of Indians. That was in 1915.

*1913
Building
a City*

The Los Angeles River at the time was incapable of such an act and the Colorado River was too far away.

La Ballona Creek came to the rescue. Canoes filled with painted savages floated on its surface. The scene was shot under the bridge at Casserini Ranch, not very far from the site of Francisco Higuera's homestead. One of the most interested spectators was Harry H. Culver.

Ince did more than shoot a scene on La Ballona Creek. He bought a piece of La Ballona Rancho. From E. P. Clark he purchased, in September 1915, a small portion of Macedonio Aguilar's allotment lying on Washington at Sixth Street, just across from the sub-division of "The Palms."

This Ince "lot" was the beginning of the Metro-Goldwyn-Mayer "lot."

Ince deeded his land to the New York Motion Picture Corporation on June 6, 1917. (For a while Keystone and Biograph pictures were produced in the plant, as well as those of the Triangle Studio—Griffith, Ince, Sennett.) Two years later Goldwyn Pictures Corporation succeeded to the title to this and adjoining property. The new owner changed its name to Gold-wyn Producing Corporation and later, on May 24, 1924, to Metro-Goldwyn-Mayer Corporation — the "M.G.M." whose name and pictures are famous throughout the world.

The Ince studio was not the first movie studio in this area, for, according to David Worsfold, historian of Palms, the Kalem Motion Picture Company had established itself in Palms during February of 1915.

An all-day carnival was held in the streets of Culver City on September 15, 1917.

The occasion? A week before, the townspeople had gone to the polls in the drug store, at 7011 Main Street, and had voted "yes" on incorporation.

1917 Incorporation

There was a parade in the morning, baseball, sideshows, booths presided over by pretty girls, fireworks in the evening, a grand ball in the club house, vaudeville and a dancing contest for the Peggy Hamilton cup.

Culver City completed its incorporation on September 20, 1917, when the board of supervisors filed its declaration with the secretary of state. The boundaries included Culver's Subdivision (Tract No. 2444), Washington Park (Tract No. 1775) and a portion of "The Palms" that had not been annexed to Los Angeles.

Carnivals were commonplace events in Culver City's first years. "What seems to attract people," Harry Culver said later, "is something moving. If an object stands still, people will not pay much attention to it." Accordingly, under the Culver tutelage, the City developed many novelty stunts to draw southern California's attention. A few of these were: a Marathon race between Los Angeles and Culver City; a baby contest with a building lot to the winner; a monthly booster parade of decorated cars, headed by a band, to a neighboring town; a picnic of trainmen to Culver City; a polo game in which Fords were substituted for horses;

a giant searchlight playing nightly from the top of the Culver City Real Estate Office; Junior Vanderbilt Cup races for boys under sixteen who had made their own cars; and a free trip around the world to the one who proposed the best name for the public park.

In 1931 the Los Angeles County Flood Control District had proposed the permanent improvement of the Ballona Channel and had included it in its county-wide flood control program.

Subsequently, under the direction of Engineer C. H. Howell, a plan for La Ballona's improvement was sub-mitted to the Federal Government. In 1935 the United States accepted the job and put it under Army engineer-ing direction.

*1935
Army
Job*

Major Theodore Wyman, Jr. sent his hundreds of workers to straighten and widen the crooked channel that since prehistoric times had been unable to hold the flood waters of rainy seasons which created lagoons and formed vast swamp areas.

They not only straightened, widened and deepened the meandering river, but they put it in a slope-sided, rock-lined strait-jacket. Also they built three bridges, with the aid of a federal grant of $800,000.00.

The result has been increased flood protection to a wide area and the reclaiming of swamp land. In addi-tion, there has been created an estuary, formed by the flow of ocean tides, extending two miles inland from the channel mouth. This makes an important rowing course. More, the work of the Army has opened up possibilities of great importance to the whole Culver

City region such as new beaches, yacht basins, and an industrial awakening to the dormant land lying between Culver City and the sea. The low land of Rancho La Ballona could well take care of textile plants and airplane factories, while a widened estuary would be a recreational center. With the cooperation of land owners affected, Culver City can work this out.

Culver City, with its eight thousand and more people, its homes, studios and industrial life, has arisen on the pasture land of the Machados and the Higueras—settlers of the Spanish period. If Augustin Machado could return today, stand on the site of his homestead and look northwest across La Ballona Creek, he would see no expanse of grassy acres dotted with cattle, but immense structures of the M. G. M. studios. Turning his back on this and looking up at the hills that once cast a shadow over his adobe, he would see them bristling with oil derricks. If Bernardo Higuera could revisit his rancho, he would find hill land covered by the charming homes of Monte Mar Vista and Cheviot Hills, by country clubs and military academies, low land covered by industrial Culver City, as well as by the studios of Selznick International and Hal Roach.

In the Pass of the Carretas—Washington Boulevard—is no longer heard the creaking of ox-drawn carts. Instead is heard the hum of auto traffic carrying thousands of studio workers and such well-known persons as Myrna Loy, Carole Lombard, Norma Shearer, Janet Gaynor, Nelson Eddy, Jeannette MacDonald, Luise

Today

Rainer, Clark Gable, Ronald Colman, Robert Taylor, Eleanor Powell, Robert Montgomery, Joan Crawford, Wallace Beery, William Powell, Spencer Tracy, Greta Garbo, Lionel Barrymore and Freddie Bartholomew. Culver City looks to the future, rather than to its rancho history. It looks to the continuing expansion of its great film industry. Especially does it look toward the sea and to well considered harbor, recreational and industrial development which will further reclaim the marsh land of La Ballona and put new life into an old rancho. With such development, Culver City, midway between Los Angeles and the ocean, can look to an abundant future.

Daniel Freeman's Horses Were Among the Best

INGLEWOOD

and the story of the
RANCHO AGUAJE DE LA CENTINELA
and the
RANCHO SAUSAL REDONDO

THE FOUNDING OF Los Angeles in 1781 brought the first white men to the Inglewood area.

The valleys and the low curving hills of what is now Inglewood lay southwest of Pueblo boundaries but they were richly grassed, the soil was black and in some of the cañadas there was abundant water. Viewed from the Baldwin Hills it was an undulating expanse of land, neutral in color, stretching seaward to the sand bluffs back of the present Playa del Rey, El Segundo and Manhattan Beach. Through it ran the Cañada del Centinela, its stream fed by perpetual springs of water.

From the beginning the citizens of Los Angeles used the region to pasture their cattle. It was better than that within their own four square leagues where no attempt had been made to mark out any community pasture land. This is the testimony of the old records.

First visitors were attracted to the springs of water —*Aguaje de la Centinela*, meaning "Sentinel Springs"— that sent up a constant flow and started a small river on its way to the ocean at Playa del Rey.

1769
Springs
of Water

Since prehistoric days the springs had been a watering place for animals. The skeleton remains of Imperial elephants and other creatures of the Pleistocene past, similar to those found in the famous Rancho La Brea pits, have been uncovered in the ancient river gravel of Centinela Park. Indians visited the place, coming from their villages near Playa del Rey and in the hills above Ballona Creek, leaving arrowheads and stone implements to be uncovered by the plows of white men. The same springs attracted the first Spanish-speaking settlers and today, still active, supply Inglewood and its thirty thousand people.

In the same year that Spanish rule in California gave way to Mexican, 1822, the first private concession of Inglewood land was made.

A citizen of the Pueblo named Antonio Ygnacio Avila was given permission by Captain Noriega, military commander at Santa Barbara, to keep his stock on the place known as the *Sausal Redondo,* which meant "Round Clump of Willows," and to build there a corral. This was on March 18, 1822, and the grant was made with the understanding that others of the Pueblo might have similar privileges by investing a similar amount of labor.

1822
Avila and
His Cattle

Avila, sometimes known as Abila, was one of five brothers who were the sons of Cornelio Avila, founder of the family and who had settled in Los Angeles in 1783. The name has always been famous in Los Angeles, partly because of the Avila adobe, belonging to one of the five, that still stands in Olvera Street.

Antonio Ygnacio Avila built a home on the ranch, possibly as early as 1826. The records give slight information, but one report to the Los Angeles City Council stated that Señor Avila had occupied the tract, with his cattle, since that year. The location of the "ruins of A. I. Abila's house" is shown on the government survey attached to the ranch patent, the site being in the present Centinela Park.

"I know the land called Sausal Redondo," said José Antonio Carrillo, prominent Pueblo citizen, in a deposition made before United States Land Commissioner Hiland Hall on November 12, 1852, "and have known it for thirty-two years. This town (Los Angeles) has been in possession of it ever since I knew it. About twenty-five or twenty-six years ago the town lent the land to Antonio Ygnacio Abila . . . I know what was recognized as the boundaries of the rancho. It is bounded on one side by the land of Dominguez, on another by the sea-coast, on the other by the land of the Machados and Tomas Sanchez and on another by the Rancho called Cuervos. Abila had a house on the land, horses and cattle and cultivated the land. He had over three thousand head of cattle and afterwards his stock was increased. The occupation of Abila and his children has continued to the present time. The house is a very good house and has been inhabited from the time the land was first occupied by Abila . . ."

At a very early date a road developed through the Inglewood region, extending from the Pueblo to the salt pond, or salt works, as it was called, near Redondo Beach. This road coincided in part with the present Redondo Boulevard and enabled Los Angeles to keep up its salt supply.

Avila claimed all of what is Inglewood in his Rancho Sausal Redondo, but presently his claim was disputed by a member of another great land-owning family, the Machado.

1833-34 Machado Comes

Don Ygnacio Machado was the first white man to settle in the cañada west of Centinela Springs.

"An honest and laborious man . . . maintains a numerous family . . . has repeatedly rendered services to the Ayuntamiento . . . a peaceable and good resident . . . is of good habits . . ."

Such were the phrases used in the old records to

describe this man who first cultivated the land of the Cañada del Centinela, or Centinela Creek, as it came to be called.

Finding the area vacant, Señor Machado moved into the cañada. He was the brother of Augustin Machado, the dominant figure on the adjoining Rancho La Ballona. In July, 1836, Ygnacio was able to report:

"I have now been cultivating the land for these three years, built two cottages, planted a vineyard of more than seven thousand stocks and sowed some Indian corn for the sustenance of my numerous family."

In addition, he built a reservoir for irrigation purposes, made ditches to conduct water, and put up a corral for the killing of stray horses of the "community."

The Ayuntamiento, or City Council, through its Committee on Vacant Lands, gave its approval to what had been done in the Cañada del Centinela. It found Don Machado supporting a mother, wife, four male children and four minor nephews. Over the protests of Avila, it gave Machado a provisional title to his ranch, with its "cornfields, vineyards and houses, without prejudicing the watering places for the cattle and horses of the community of the City, as the City has not marked the common belonging to it."

In May of 1837, Governor Alvarado, in the name of the Mexican nation, granted the Ranch of the Round Clump of Willows to Antonio Ygnacio Avila.

In September of 1844, another governor, Michel-

1844
Provisional
Title
torena, in the name of the Mexican nation, gave Machado provisional title to Aguaje de la Centinela "from the
spring 'Ojo de Agua' to the Indian corn."

The most northerly boundary of the ranch, as finally established by United States survey, is the present
line of Centinela Avenue. At its most southerly point
it reached what is now Buckthorn Street.

All of the present-day Inglewood lies within the
Ranchos Sausal Redondo and Aguaje de la Centinela,
as their boundaries were finally established by United
States government surveyors, except the portion north
of Centinela Avenue and also certain eastern portions
which were held to be public land.

On April 7, 1845, Ygnacio Machado conveyed his
ranch to Bruno Avila, 57-year-old brother of the owner
of the Sausal Redondo.

1845
Barrels of
Aguardiente
Machado, then 54, gave up the property he had
developed and that for a dozen years had been his home.
In addition he presented the new owner with two bar-
rels of aguardiente, containing one hundred and fifty
pints each, a "good sample of this year's crop."

In exchange Machado got Pueblo property consist-
ing of a small tract of land with a vineyard, a three-
room house and two corrals.

Thus the two Avila brothers, Bruno and Antonio,
came to own all of the area upon which Inglewood was
to rise.

California became a part of the United States in
1848 and two years later it was admitted to the Union
as a state.

The Avila brothers filed their petitions with the Board of Land Commissioners in 1852. This Board had been created a year before to pass upon Mexican land titles. Bruno's title was confirmed in 1854 and Antonio's in 1855. The United States District Court upheld the Board and government patents were issued the claimants during President Grant's administration.

The patent for Aguaje de la Centinela, containing over 2200 acres, was dated August 23, 1872, and that for Sausal Redondo, containing about 22,500 acres, March 22, 1875.

The owner of the Centinela Springs needed money more than land. In July of 1851 he went to James P. McFarland and John G. Downey, prominent land owners and merchants, and borrowed $400.00. A few years later he borrowed $1400 more, this time from Hilliard P. Dorsey. To secure these borrowings he mortgaged his home and his ranch. He put on three mortgages, each with interest at 6% per *month*.

*1851
Bruno Signs
a Mortgage*

Avila couldn't pay back the money he had borrowed and the holders of all three mortgages rushed in to foreclose. Avila and his wife contested the foreclosure and were able to defeat McFarland and Downey, the District Court holding that Señora Avila's failure to sign the mortgage on the homestead nullified the mortgage itself.

Dorsey, the other mortgage holder, had better luck. In spite of Señora Avila's claim that she and her husband understood Spanish only, that the mortgage had not been explained to her and that she supposed part of the ranch had been reserved, a $3300 judgment and decree of foreclosure was obtained.

1856
Auction
Sale
Hilliard P. Dorsey stood in front of the County Court House in Los Angeles and bid in Bruno's ranch for $2000. This was $1300 less than the amount of the decree, showing that a deficiency judgment is not a modern invention. Six months later the Sheriff gave him a deed.

Dorsey, the new owner, was a southerner, a veteran of the Mexican War. He had married Civility Rubottom, daughter of Uncle Billy Rubottom, later famous for his tavern at Spadra where the stages changed horses. He and his wife and his wife's relatives had their disagreements.

One day the owner of Centinela went to El Monte, where his wife and baby had gone and where Rubottom then lived. Captain Dorsey carried a pistol and Uncle Billy a shot-gun. The shot-gun got into play first and Dorsey was killed.

Dorsey's widow found ranch ownership burdensome. There were disputes as to boundaries and water privileges. A certain Frenchman, too, a son-in-law of Bruno Avila, would not give up possession. It was a relief to her to be able to sell the property to Francis J. Carpenter who almost immediately transferred the ranch over to the attorney and land title expert, Joseph Lancaster Brent. The amount paid by Carpenter for his deed to the whole of Aguaje de la Centinela was $930.00. This was the balance due on a contract of

purchase entered into with Hilliard P. Dorsey for
$3000. Attorney Brent quickly settled the Avila prob-
lem by paying $300 to Bruno's son-in-law for a waiver
of claims.

Just before the outbreak of the Civil War, Sir
Robert Burnett, of Crathe's Castle, Scotland, arrived
in Los Angeles County. He brought with him some
money and a wish to be a ranchero. He was ready
to exchange green, misty Scotland for warm, romantic
California.

1860
Sir Robert
Burnett

The owners of two ranches were glad to accommodate the newcomer. Joseph Lancaster Brent sold him
Rancho Aguaje de la Centinela, with its wonderful
springs, for $3000, just what Brent had originally paid.

The heirs of Antonio Ygnacio Avila (he having
died in 1858) sold the magnificent Rancho Sausal Redondo to Burnett for approximately $30,000.

Sir Robert at once took possession of his 25,000-
acre domain. For his home he took the old Bruno
Avila adobe that still stands, one of the charming spots
in Inglewood. It lay west of the springs and overlooked
the Cañada del Centinela, the adobe whose first bricks
may have been laid by Ygnacio Machado. From the
cool retreat of this low, rambling house, with its four-
foot walls, its patio and its garden, he directed operations on his vast acreage.

Like his predecessors Burnett devoted the Centinela Ranch to sheep and cattle raising.

After a dozen years or more as ranchero, the owner

of the Centinela found it necessary to return to Scotland. He looked about for someone to take over the ranch.

Daniel Freeman was that "someone." He was a Canadian who had decided upon a trip to Jamaica for his wife's health, but had come instead to California after reading Charles Nordhoff's "California: For Health, Pleasure and Residence," a popular book of the Seventies.

Freeman inspected a number of southern California ranches, including those in the San Gabriel and San Fernando Valleys. One day he went over the Centinela with Sir Robert. The cool sea air, he felt, would benefit Mrs. Freeman's health. This converted him, along with the rolling hills, the fertile cañadas, the abundant springs and the view of the Santa Monica Mountains that rose in a blue wall to the northwest. He not only wanted to manage the ranch, he wanted to be its owner.

"I'll take a lease on the place," the man who later would be called the father of Inglewood told Burnett, "provided you'll give me an option to buy."

*1873
Daniel
Freeman*

On April 19, 1873, a lease was drawn up. It named Freeman's wife, Catherine Grace Higginson Freeman, as lessee. The document was recorded and may be examined by anyone. It provided for a yearly rental of $7500. By separate agreement an option of buying Centinela was given for $150,000.00.

The Freemans, including the three children, went to live in the old adobe that had been Burnett's home and the ranch took on new life.

Freeman re-stocked Centinela with sheep.

To carry out Sir Robert's plans he put out 1500 eucalyptus and pepper trees. He followed this up by planting 7000 orange trees, 1800 lemons, 2000 almonds, 400 lime and 300 olive trees. Back of this activity were the ever-flowing sources of underground water, aided by wells and windmills.

Since the Thirties Centinela had seen much of sheep and cattle raising. Now it was to go in for horse raising, and Freeman's horses were among the best. The Freeman children had horses to ride. In spring they could ride all day through the fields of wild flowers that extended from the adobe to the ocean, meeting no one except ranch employees. There were poppies, lupin, wild mustard, wild horseradish and finally the pink verbena of the sand dunes.

Unfortunately Mrs. Freeman did not long enjoy the Centinela Ranch that had been acquired to give her health. When she died in November of 1874, her husband was left to carry the burden alone and to bring up three children: Archibald Christie Freeman, Charles Freeman and Grace Elizabeth Isabella Freeman.

Two seasons without rain brought terrific losses to the cattle and sheep men of southern California. While some owners were driving their herds over the cliffs at Santa Monica and San Pedro, Daniel Freeman sent his sheep into the mountains. At that he lost twenty-two thousand head.

As a result of the drought Freeman came to the same conclusion that Colonel Lankershim did in the

San Fernando Valley. He would go in for dry farming, and turn Centinela into a barley ranch.

And so, in due time, the golden fields of Aguaje de la Centinela and of Sausal Redondo, with their close-packed stalks of barley, stretched away toward the sea. The first planting of 640 acres yielded 25 bushels to the acre. The plantings were extended and by 1880 Centinela was producing a million bushels a year, some of which were shipped to New York and London.

Twelve years after he had leased the great ranch Daniel Freeman got a deed. On May 4, 1885, Sir Robert Burnett and Matilda Josephine, Lady Burnett, executed the final instrument that transferred title to Freeman. The recorded document shows a consideration of $140,-000.00. A few years before, Freeman had obtained a deed to a portion for $22,243.00.

The Centinela-Inglewood Land Company was organized in 1887 by a group of men who could picture a town springing up out of a barley field.

This organization, destined to preside at the birth of Inglewood, had as its first directors and organizers:

Charles Silent, Los Angeles
Dan McFarland, Los Angeles
N. R. Vail, Los Angeles
L. J. Rose, Los Angeles
E. C. Webster, Pasadena
L. T. Garnsey, Los Angeles
W. N. Monroe, Monrovia

The purposes of the corporation, as announced in its articles, were:

" . . . To lay out, survey and map villages, towns and cities; and to buy and sell the lots and blocks or subdivisions; . . . to erect and maintain hotel or other buildings and water and gas works, pipes, mains, reservoirs, and appliances within or for the benefit of such villages, towns or cities . . ."

Purchasing a large acreage from Daniel Freeman, the corporation took steps to carry out these purposes.

A name for the unborn town had already been selected: "Inglewood," suggested, some say, by Inglewood in Canada, others by Englewood near Chicago.

During the months of August and September, 1887, surveyors laid out the new town, keeping it close to the source of water, the Centinela Springs.

1887 New Town

With the completion of a railroad to Redondo Beach, by way of Inglewood, in the spring of 1888, there was nothing to stop the boom plans for a city.

A lumber company announced in the first issue of "The Inglewood Star" on April 21, 1888, that:

"1,500,000 feet of lumber will be delivered at Inglewood at once. 4,500,000 feet more coming. Lumber will be sold at cost to all who build . . . 50 new buildings going up inside of thirty days."

The Centinela-Inglewood Land Company offered residence lots at $200 to $500 each, business lots at $250 to $750, orchard lots at $600 to $1500, and acreage at $200 to $400 an acre.

Eleven miles of water pipe were laid, and already

there had sprung up two grocery stores, a planing mill, a wagon repair shop, a drug store, a livery stable, a butcher shop, a brick yard, five real estate offices and ambitious plans for the Freeman College of Applied Sciences.

A large frame hotel had been put up—without which no boom town in the Eighties was complete. For its opening there was announced a grand house-warming, a supper and ball given under the auspices of the Inglewood Floral Company, and a special night train chartered to carry invited guests to and from Los Angeles.

"Hold up! Hold up! Have you seen Inglewood?" ran the ads of the real estate men of the day, but the official announcement told the full story. It read:

"Inglewood is ready to welcome the home-seeker. She offers many attractions that are not to be found elsewhere. She is near Los Angeles. She is near the Pacific Ocean—so near that on quiet evenings the roar of the surf beating on its shore can be heard in the town. Her streets are wide thoroughfares, well graded and lined with shade trees. Her water supply is piped to and from an immense reservoir. A public park, irregular in shape, but following the bend of a creek flowing the year round with spring water, winds through the heart of the town, and divides it into two parts. Her educational facilities are to be of the best character, and she is to have in her midst a richly endowed college of Applied

Sciences, the building of which is to be commenced this Spring. She is the center of a farming region comprising about eleven thousand acres of very fertile soil. She is going to grow into a large, beautiful and prosperous town. Town lots and farms in and near Inglewood are to be bought cheap today. They will never be cheaper, for Inglewood is not a town on paper."

Today a city of more than thirty thousand people has arisen about Centinela Springs, whose waters have been flowing since prehistoric days.

Aguaje de la Centinela was responsible for the   Today *planting of the first vineyards and the first cornfields by Don Ygnacio Machado one hundred years ago. It made possible the birth of the town of Inglewood fifty years later. Its water sources today supply the needs of a city whose homes, buildings and factories cover the undulating fields and fill the cañadas that pastured the horses of the first citizens of the Pueblo of Los Angeles.*

Inglewood, the retail business, manufacturing and airport center of the large population area that was once a sheep and cattle ranch, then a barley ranch, recalls with interest and pride the men whose good sense led them to the Springs of Centinela and the men whose energy developed the region served by the Springs.

Selling Lots in the Seventies

SANTA MONICA

and the story of the
RANCHO SAN VICENTE Y SANTA MONICA

IN AUGUST OF 1769 white men stood on or near the site of Santa Monica. They were scouts of the Portolá party that had begun the occupation and exploration of California for Spain. These Spaniards looked down upon the rolling surf. They saw the mountains of Malibu lifting up into the haze.

Then they returned to their camp at an Indian village located where two springs rose from a hollow in

144

the hills near the present Soldiers' Home at Sawtelle. They reported to the others who stayed behind that they had reached a high, steep cliff, "terminating in the sea where the mountains end," and that passage north along the shore was cut off. So the Portolá party, bound for Monterey, decided to avoid the beach. It followed Sepulveda Canyon to the summit of the Santa Monica range and down into the San Fernando Valley.

1769
Scouts
of Portolá

When California became Mexican, Santa Monica was still an unoccupied and unclaimed mesa covered with wild grass.

There were visitors, however, for the Malibu Rancho, lying northwesterly of Topanga Canyon, had been given in 1805 to José Bartolome Tapia. Smugglers, too, found the isolated coast convenient. And in the adjoining canyons Indians had huts among the sycamores by the streams.

In 1828, Francisco Sepulveda, soldier and Los Angeles citizen, was given possession of and provisional title to "the place called San Vicente." San Vicente included all of the original town of Santa Monica. It faced the ocean, extending from the Canyon to what is now Pico Boulevard. In the rear it reached almost to the Westwood region and took in the mountains that overlooked the San Fernando Valley.

The grant was given him, Sepulveda explained later, not only because he was the owner of more than one hundred and fifty head of horned cattle, but because of his "having been an old soldier of the country and having worked at the most painful period, when wan-

dering amidst nomadic tribes, suffering untold priva-
tions and in constant danger of life." Sepulveda was
not only a soldier, but the son of a soldier, for his father
was one of the troops that came with the first settlers
to Los Angeles in 1781. The son was then a boy of six.

1827-28
Settlers

Sepulveda was officially put in possession by José
Antonio Carrillo, then alcalde of Los Angeles and the
representative of the state government.

The year before that, in 1827, Xavier Alvarado and
Antonio Machado had been given a provisional grant
of "the place called Santa Monica." "Santa Monica"
then referred to the Canyon and the land that lay between it and Topanga Canyon, extending to the hills
in the rear—territory mostly outside present-day Santa
Monica.

In 1831, Machado gave up his interest to Alvarado,
and when Alvarado died his sons remained in possession
until 1838 when they abandoned "Santa Monica" in
favor of Ysidro Reyes and Francisco Marquez. Even
today representatives of the Reyes and Marquez families live in Santa Monica and have retained a part of
the rancho they once owned.

The owners of the two ranchos brought cattle,
horses and sheep to their new land. Sepulveda, who
lived in town, built an adobe house near the springs,
called San Vicente Springs, where the Portolá party
had stopped. He set out orchards and vineyards. His
sons, too, built houses.

Reyes established himself on the bluff of the Huntington Palisades. Later he moved across the Canyon

that his sheep might have better protection from the wolves. He put up what is said to be the first house on the site of the city of Santa Monica. It stood near the spot where Seventh Street now dips into the Canyon, with a full view of the sea. Marquez built farther down in the Canyon and some of his descendants still live within a stone's throw of the home place.

The grant to Francisco Sepulveda was confirmed by Governor Alvarado in December, 1839. Sepulveda promptly lost his title papers, so later on, in 1846, Pio Pico had to come to the rescue with another grant.

In the same year of 1839 began the lengthy dispute between the Sepulvedas, on the one side, and the Reyes and the Marquez families on the other. Both claimed "Santa Monica," or "Boca de Santa Monica," as it was also called, the magnificent pasture land that stretched between the Santa Monica and Topanga Canyons. "Boca" means "mouth."

1839
Title
Disputes

Sepulveda insisted that this strip was properly an annex of his larger grant of San Vicente.

"Without it," he said, "I have no place for my horses and am reduced to a piece of land where I eke out a miserable existence."

The leading citizens of Los Angeles took sides. Carrillo, Dominguez and Talamantes lined up with Sepulveda. Machado and Lugo went with Reyes and Marquez. Petitions were addressed to governors. Courts were appealed to. Trips were made to Monterey.

Ultimately Sepulveda lost the disputed land, but he gained the name. He had been calling his ranch San

Vicente *and* Santa Monica so long that the name stuck.
And the Americans dropped "San Vicente."

To help Reyes and Marquez, Antonio Machado,
then alcalde, went to Santa Monica, accompanied by
chain bearers. He began his survey at the mouth of
Topanga Canyon. He had with him a cord one hundred varas long (a vara being thirty-three inches), to
the end of which was attached two small billets of wood.
He and his aides started down the beach, measuring
seventy-five hundred varas to a point in the first ravine
just southeast of Santa Monica Canyon. Here Don Fernando Sepulveda appeared, on behalf of his father,
Francisco. Together they proceeded to throw the
cord from south to north. They got tired and very
hot. Finally, when they had reached the bottom of a
deep mountain ravine, they decided the country was
too rough. They marked a dead tree with a machete
and did the rest of the surveying on paper. The result
was the "Diseño de Santa Hermonica." Its date was
1839.

In 1843, Don Juan Warner made a survey for Sepulveda. He happened to have a compass and a two-
hundred-vara cord and did not avoid the mountains,
so produced a fairly good map.

California was admitted as a state to the Union two
years after Mexico ceded it by treaty. Then, in 1851,
the Board of Land Commissioners was created to investigate and pass upon land titles. The owners of the
two ranchos filed their petitions with this Board soon

after its creation, but thirty years went by before all questions of title and survey were settled.

Finally, in 1881, United States patents were issued. To the widow of Francisco Sepulveda went "Rancho San Vicente y Santa Monica," with thirty thousand acres. To Ysidro Reyes *et al* went "Boca de Santa Monica," with sixty-six hundred acres.

When Don Francisco Sepulveda died in 1853 he willed Santa Monica to his widow, Ramona.

*1853
Sepulveda's
Will*

"In the name of God, beginning and ending of all things," the will began, "know all persons who may see this will—that I, Francisco Sepulveda, a native of the town of Sinaloa, in the Republic of Mexico, the legitimate son of Francisco Xavier Sepulveda and of Maria Candelaria Arredondo, residents of the same place (may they rest in peace), finding myself in bad health but not seriously ill . . . that I have ten children alive and two dead . . . it is my desire that as soon as I die I may be buried in the cemetery of this City of Los Angeles, after having performed the requisites and ceremonies of the Church . . . I declare that I am the owner of Rancho San Vicente . . . that I own three houses and an orchard on the said rancho . . . of these houses two have only one room apiece and the other has two rooms and a back yard . . . that I have about 500 head of neat cattle . . . about 50 head of sheep . . . a house and furniture in the City of Los

Angeles, in which I reside, situate in the corner of the principal plaza . . . that Juan Pollorena owes me three gentle cows . . . that I owe Juan Warner $11 in money that he loaned me . . . that my eldest son José and my son Dolores I name as my executors . . . that the bulk of my estate I leave to my wife Ramona Serrano as my sole and general heiress, without any person having any reason to trouble or molest her in any manner and leaving her without any obligation from me other than to deliver to my son Dolores 150 cows . . ."

For several years before 1872, Santa Monica Canyon had been used as a summer resort. The Reyes and Marquez families were very tolerant of visitors. Campers from Los Angeles enjoyed the sycamores and surf-bathing. Saturday night dances were held in a big tent. Bonfires blazed.

On the mesa itself, site of the unborn town of Santa Monica, a trail crossed the grass-covered prairie to the foot of what is Colorado Avenue. It was used by the ox-teams that hauled brea from the Hancock Ranch tar pits on Rancho La Brea to a little wharf that extended into the ocean. Boats took the brea to San Francisco.

1872
Colonel
Baker

Colonel R. S. Baker, who had been in the cattle business in the Tejon country and before that had come to San Francisco from Rhode Island in 1849, made a trip to Santa Monica. He looked over the flat expanse, with its one house, and decided it would make a good sheep ranch. He went to the Sepulveda heirs and paid them

$55,000 for their rancho. Later he bought part of the Reyes-Marquez property adjoining on the northwest and also part of La Ballona or Machado Rancho adjoining San Vicente on the southeast. He stocked his new land with sheep.

Senator John P. Jones of Nevada, a man of wealth, appeared on the scene in 1874 and Colonel Baker sold him a three-fourths interest in his ranch for $162,500. Together they planned a railroad, a wharf and a town.

On July 10, 1875, a map of "Santa Monica, Cal." was recorded in the office of the County Recorder at Los Angeles. The townsite fronted on the ocean and was bounded on the northwest by Montana Avenue, on the southeast by Railroad Avenue (now Colorado) and on the northeast by 26th Street.

A few days later the first sale of lots was held. It was much advertised. A steamer brought people from San Francisco and stages brought others from Los Angeles for the great occasion.

Tom Fitch was the orator of the day and the auctioneer of lots. Jones had agreed to give him one-fifth of his interest in the entire town and ranch for $47,000 —"to be paid out of the proceeds of the sales of lots and lands." On that hot July day there was no shade on the Santa Monica townsite and the air was filled with the dust made by buggies, wagons, stages, horses and men. Fitch did his best. He talked about the Pacific Ocean being draped with a western sky of scarlet and gold, about a bay filled with white-winged ships, about a frostless, bracing, warm yet un-languid air, odored

*1875
Auction of
Town Lots*

with the breath of flowers. The title to the land, he said, would be guaranteed by the owners and the title to the ocean, the sunset and the air by God.

Harris Newmark bid in the first lot at $300. Fitch let him take four others at the same price, all on Ocean Avenue.

Within nine months Santa Monica had a thousand people and a hundred and sixty houses. The Los Angeles and Independence Railroad, sponsored by Senator Jones, was built to Los Angeles and was planned to be part of a great transcontinental system with western terminus at Santa Monica. A wharf was finished. A reservoir was constructed, with water for the town coming from San Vicente Springs. The same year saw a school district organized, a church established, the beginnings of a public library, a bathhouse, a hotel and the first number of the first newspaper, the Santa Monica Outlook.

Santa Monica was on its way.

1887 Sub-divisions

Santa Monica shared in the excitement of the Great Boom that swept Southern California in 1887. It went in heavily for new subdivisions, land auctions, better train service and more hotels—including the handsome Arcadia, named after Colonel Baker's wife, to whom he had deeded all his interest in Santa Monica.

In 1888 Senator Jones and Mrs. Baker presented a deed of three hundred acres to the "National Home for Disabled Volunteer Soldiers." This was followed by the erection of barracks, hospital and buildings for a thousand men. It brought business to the merchants of Santa Monica and started the town of Sawtelle.

In 1891-92 the long wharf at "Port Los Angeles," north of Santa Monica, was built. The shipping and trade that had been lost when the earlier railroad and harbor plans collapsed were regained. But the long wharf and "Port Los Angeles" were temporary, and when Santa Monica emerged from its disappointments it found itself destined to be a residence city and an unexcelled beach resort. Today citizens congratulate themselves on the turn of events.

By agreement between the Town of Santa Monica, Senator Jones and Mrs. Baker and by order of court, the ocean-front strip of land on top of the bluff was dedicated to the public in 1892. This perpetuated Santa Monica's palisades as a park and the city's beauty as a seaside resort.

The 1905 population of Santa Monica was 7200. In October of that year a board of freeholders was elected to draft a charter. The year following, the charter was ratified at public election and the State Legislature gave its approval in 1907.

1907
City
Charter

The original townsite had long since overspread its boundaries and on the southeast had gone far beyond Pico Boulevard into La Ballona Rancho.

By legislative act, approved April 10, 1917, the State of California granted to the city of Santa Monica the tide lands and the submerged lands bordering upon and below the mean high tide line. This made the City's waterfront activities possible, including its breakwater and yacht harbor.

For a few years following 1920 the influx of people to southern California was a flood, with every state in the union contributing to the western migration. Santa Monica shared in this distribution of prosperity and population. Building activity continued and today Santa Monica has handsome beach clubs along the strand and distinguished homes throughout the city and in the canyons and hills around. The city's superb setting attracted writers, painters and sculptors.

1935
Saint
Monica

Where Wilshire Boulevard ends at the Palisades, Santa Monica placed a sculptured figure of the saint after whom was named the bay, the ranch and the city. It is the work of Eugene Morahan.

This sculpture revives a legend of the origin of the name of the city: that the first Spanish explorers, looking upon the springs (San Vicente) where they camped, thought of the sparkling tears of Saint Monica who wept for her wayward son, Augustine, and thereupon named the place Santa Monica.

The diaries of these explorers, unfortunately, do not bear out the story. The old archives and maps indicate that the name Santa Monica was first applied to the stream flowing through Santa Monica Canyon, then to the land northwest of the Canyon, and finally to the mesa where the City now stands. Its origin, however, is shrouded in haze like the golden mist that hangs on late afternoons over the boundary mountains.

Santa Monica's waters today are as placid, the curve of the bay as lovely and the mountains as luminous as when Cabrillo and his men cast anchor one October day in 1542.

Today

The white beach and the tawny cliffs are as impressive now as when Tom Fitch talked about them in 1875.

Once a pasture land, then a struggling village, today a city of fifty-five thousand, Santa Monica looks to an abundant future.

The Last Indian Raid

BEVERLY HILLS

and the story of the
RANCHO RODEO DE LAS AGUAS

IN AUGUST OF 1769 a cavalcade of men, horses and mules on its way north passed through what is now Beverly Hills.

Don Gaspar de Portolá, Spanish governor of the Californias, headed the party. He and his soldiers, sweating in their leather jackets, were the first white men to follow the Indian trail that is now Wilshire Boulevard in Los Angeles. They were the first to see the boiling brea pits, famous today for their Pleistocene

156

animal deposits. They crossed a wide plain rising to canyons and hillsides that are now patterned with the homes of men and women famous "in pictures." They looked up at the rich, dark forms of hills bearing away toward the sea. They crossed the beds of nearly dry streams lined with sycamores. They saw the green carpets made by ciénegas or swamps and that night (August 3, 1769) they camped at the "Spring of the Alders of San Estevan."

Following the famous march of Portolá through California, presidios, missions and pueblos were established. Soldiers, priests and colonists came north from Mexico.

Colonists for Los Angeles, the unborn pueblo, were recruited in Sonora and Sinaloa. They made the long, hard journey north to San Gabriel in 1781.

Among them was Luis Quintero, a tailor, who, with his wife, enlisted at Los Alamos in Sonora. Quintero's son-in-law, Eugenio Valdez, came along with the same expedition for he was one of the soldier guard. The soldier's fifteen-year-old wife, Sebastiana Quintero, was in the party too. Then there was Vicente Ferrer Villa, a six-year-old boy who came to California, by a different route, with his parents and another group of settlers. They chose to follow the Anza trail from the presidio of Tubac in Sonora, over the Colorado Desert and on to San Gabriel.

1781
Three
Adventurers

The fortunes of these three adventurers, the tailor, the soldier and the boy, are linked with those of Beverly Hills' first settler: Maria Rita Valdez.

Quintero was her grandfather. Valdez was her father. And Vicente Villa grew up and became her husband.

Just when Maria Rita Valdez and her soldier husband, whom she married in 1808, came to live in Beverly Hills is not disclosed by the records.

It may have been before 1822, the year that Spanish rule gave way to Mexican. Testimony given later before the United States Land Commission indicates this.

José Antônio Carrillo testified that Sergeant Villa of "the Spanish army" was retired "as an invalid with a pension" and that "when he left the service he went to live on this land."

"This land," of which Carrillo spoke, was the Rancho Rodeo de las Aguas, now Beverly Hills. He recalled visiting it, as Alcalde of Los Angeles, on a boundary matter in 1828. He told of finding the ranch occupied by Maria Rita Valdez and her large family.

"Rodeo de las Aguas"—the gathering of the waters—was derived from the meeting of streams that in the rainy months rushed down Cold Water and Benedict Canyons, creating a chain of lakes and swamps in the lower lands that extended across the plain.

1828
Maria Rita
a Widow

After Villa's death in 1828 the widow, left with eleven children, was to find ranch ownership, even in Beverly Hills, a burden.

". . . In the year 1831"—so the old records of Los Angeles read—"Citizen Vicente Sanchez, being the Alcalde of this town, granted to her (Maria Rita Valdez) jointly with Luciano Valdez (her kinsman) a tract of land called San Antonio . . ."

A picture of the ranch at this time has come down to us, drawn by Francisco Villa testifying twenty years later.

"When I first knew it in 1833," he explained, "it was occupied by Maria Rita Valdez and a relative of hers, Luciano Valdez. She had cattle on the land but not one hundred and fifty head of cattle, which was necessary at that time to entitle her to a grant of land and to have a brand for cattle. This mission of San Gabriel of which I was major-domo, lent her sufficient to make up that number. She also had horses. She built a house on the land the same year, in which she lived and still continues living there. She has two small houses on the land . . . There are two ditches on the place, but very little water. She has cultivated a small garden. There are three small springs from which one of the ditches runs and the other ditch runs from a swamp . . . The name of the rancho in the title from Governor Alvarado was San Antonio, it had been before called Rodeo de las Aguas. She gave it the name of San Antonio . . ."

The house Maria Rita built stood somewhere near the present northwest corner of Sunset Boulevard and Alpine Drive. If she could return today she would find that across Sunset Wallace Beery was occupying a white and green California-Colonial mansion. Other close neighbors would be James Gleason, Edward G. Robinson, Josephine Hutchinson, Corinne Griffith and Gloria Swanson. And to get to her house she would have to pass by the homes of Richard Barthelmess, Adrienne Ames, Conrad Nagel and others of the picture world.

Maria Rita Valdez was soon to find that a 4500-acre ranch is altogether too small for two people if one of them is Luciano.

It was fortunate for Maria Rita Valdez de Villa that she had a town house in Los Angeles as well as the one she had built on her ranch.

1834
Bad
Neighbor
By 1834 she was pleading with Governor Figueroa for relief from her unruly neighbor and kinsman, Luciano, who, incidentally, had been the pueblo's schoolmaster from 1827 to 1830.

Luciano moved his house too close—closer than 70 feet—obstructing the front of her home. He ran her cattle off the only watering place in the whole ranch, though he had almost no cattle of his own. So her animals went wandering over into the ranchos of her neighbors, Rocha, Higuera and Alanis. Luciano said he owned a certain cañada that she had spent three months clearing. He would not let her plant vines when she wanted to plant them. He dared her to complain to anyone. He was overproud of his ability to read and write. He suffered from "bad temper," used "indecent language" and was "intolerable."

The widow Valdez' complaint was turned over to the Los Angeles City Council or Ayuntamiento. What Luciano said about Maria is not disclosed, but the Council promptly ordered Luciano to vacate the premises, not only because of the discord in Beverly Hills but because he lacked the required number of cattle to entitle him to ownership.

This fight did not end immediately, for Maria Rita had to pay Luciano for the property he was giving up. Two skilled appraisers were appointed, Jesus Diaz, representing the widow, and Tomas Talamantes, Luciano. They went forth to the great ranch, put a value of fifteen dollars on Luciano's house, two dollars on a peach tree and a half a dollar on "two poles for farming purposes," a grand total of $17.50. A settlement agreement was drawn up in the presence of the Mayor and other prominent citizens. Finally on August 11, 1844, the sum of $17.50 was turned over to Luciano and the ten-year dispute was ended.

Twenty-nine people lived on Rancho Rodeo de las Aguas in 1836, as shown by the first census of the Los Angeles District. Their ages ranged from one to fifty. Most of them bore the names of Valdez, Villa or Vejar. Among them was Ricardo Vejar who later settled the Pomona Valley. The number does not include the owner of the place, for Maria Rita Valdez was listed by the same census as living in Los Angeles, a widow aged 50.

A messenger from the widow Valdez, Captain Villa,

1836 Census

set out one morning for Monterey to see Governor Alvarado. He carried with him a petition.

On the way he stopped at San Juan Bautista where José Castro, the Prefect of the District, lived. General Castro was an old friend of Maria Rita, for he and several of his officers had boarded at her Los Angeles house when the troops were south. Castro was asked to use his influence with the Governor.

The two rode on to Monterey and, with Castro at his elbow, Alvarado signed everything his visitors wanted.

Captain Villa returned to Los Angeles and gave Maria Rita the title papers for her Rancho Rodeo de las Aguas.

In her house on Main Street, Los Angeles, Maria Rita had a trunk. In that trunk she kept her valuables, including the title papers and grant which the Governor had signed at Monterey.

When the Americans, under Commodore Stockton, marched into Los Angeles in 1846, hoisting a new flag in place of the Mexican, many citizens fled the town. Among them were Maria Rita Valdez and members of her family.

1846 Trunk Rifled

While the house stood vacant it was pillaged, according to Maria, and her trunk "rifled by some unknown party either of Californians, Indians or Americans." The title papers were taken, never to be returned.

California came into the United States by the Treaty of Guadalupe Hidalgo and on September 9, 1850, was admitted as a state to the Union.

Maria Rita Valdez filed her ranch claims with the Board of United States Land Commissioners on November 11, 1852.

Not having any title papers to prove her claims she had to rely on the testimony of relatives and friends who were summoned before the Board.

Her son Mariano, who looked after his mother's interest in the ranch, told of living on the place since 1832. He said his mother had kept it cultivated ever since with the exception of the two years when his brother-in-law was in charge.

José Antonio Carrillo came forward with his usual good memory.

Former Governor Alvarado was called, but Alvarado suffered from a very bad memory.

Then General Castro was put on the stand.

"I went and saw the Governor," he said, "and asked his favorable attention . . . and the Governor issued the title . . . which he gave to me, in my own hand, granting to said Doña Maria Rita about one league of land."

Maria Rita's claim was confirmed by the Board on September 25, 1855, and its decision was affirmed in June of 1857 on appeal to the United States District Court.

During Grant's administration, on June 27, 1871, the patent was issued.

Three Indians, hiding behind a sycamore tree in the rear of Maria Rita's ranch house, opened fire at the occupants one day in 1852. For several hours the siege lasted, with the besieged returning the Indians' fire.

1852 Indians Open Fire

When Maria Rita's ammunition was running low, a nine-year-old boy slipped out the front door unnoticed, crawled along a shallow ditch for half a mile and then dashed on to the Sherman region for help.

Ranchers on horseback came to the rescue. They chased the Indians to a walnut grove near the present Beverly Hills Women's Club site. There they shot and buried them.

The last Indian raid in the Los Angeles area took place in April of 1853, but Rancho Rodeo de las Aguas suffered no loss. Coming horseback through the Cahuenga Pass, the raiders swept through the Hollywood, Beverly Hills and Westwood regions. They crossed the Rancho La Brea, teeming with horses, crossed Maria Rita's ranch and on to the pasture lands of the Rancho San José de Buenos Ayres. Here they helped themselves to Don Benito Wilson's fat cattle and, driving the stolen animals ahead, retraced their way, unmolested.

*1854
Ranch
Sold*

In 1854 two Americans came along with five hundred dollars cash and bought Beverly Hills and more besides. In addition to the cash, they gave notes amounting to $500 and agreed that when the United States confirmed the title they would pay $300 more.

Maria Rita gave the newcomers a deed to the Villa Ranch, as the Rancho Rodeo de las Aguas was unromantically called. Along with the land went "four houses built of adobe."

One of the purchasers was Benjamin D. Wilson—the famous Don Benito—neighbor on the west. The other was Henry Hancock, whose family bought

Rancho La Brea on the east. Now, with their combined ranches, they hoped to turn a plain into a vast wheat field.

The last payment on the Villa ranch was not made for many years, not until after Maria Rita's death. A marginal note on the deed shows that on January 10, 1869, a note in favor of Rita Valdez de Villa was "paid out in coin to her heirs."

The plans of Don Benito Wilson and of William Workman (who had succeeded to Hancock's title) failed.

Wilson had planted 2000 acres to wheat in 1862 and had built a three-room adobe near Maria Rita's old home. The first year there had been good crops. But the two seasons that followed were dry. The swamps disappeared and no wild geese flew over the brown reed grass. No lupin or poppies bloomed in the spring. Rodeo de las Aguas became a withered plain instead of a wheat ranch.

There was a brief oil boom in 1865, with the Los Angeles Pioneer Oil Company buying oil rights and drilling wells.

1865 Oil Boom

In the late Sixties the Basque sheep herders began to drift in. The names of Amestoy and Domaleche are of this period.

Other newcomers appeared to farm and to raise sheep.

In 1866 James Whitworth for $1150 bought 125 acres lying north of the present Pico and between Robertson and La Ciénega Boulevards. A giant eucalyptus tree standing today on Robertson, near Pico, in a district of homes, shops and stores, remains a monument to Whitworth and the Whitworth ranch.

In 1868, Edson A. Benedict, a Los Angeles storekeeper who had come from Missouri, filed a claim in one of the canyons just outside of the Rancho. It has since been known as Benedict Canyon. At its mouth he built his home. Later his son, Pierce E. Benedict, acquired land adjoining and put up a house. The Benedicts planted walnut trees, beans and other vegetables and raised bees. Other settlers came into Benedict Canyon. Today its winding road is lined with homes.

"Purchase of five acres of wooded property in Benedict Canyon," a recent newspaper clipping reads, "was completed during the week by Bill Cagney, brother and business manager of Jimmy Cagney, motion picture star . . . It is understood that Cagney is preparing to have the five acres fully landscaped and will erect a dwelling there."

*1868
Benedict
and Preuss*

In the same year, 1868, that the first Benedict came to Beverly Hills, a wool dealer named Edward A. Preuss became the owner of Rancho Rodeo de las Aguas. He bought the whole ranch, minus the Whitworth parcel, from Wilson and Workman, for $10,775.00.

Preuss was interested in sheep, farming and athletics. One of the early maps of the ranch shows the barley fields of Preuss extending from the road that is Pico north to the hills.

Other early settlers on the Rancho Rodeo de las Aguas were George P. Ruhland, Frederick L. Buhn and F. X. Eberle, who bought land from Preuss in 1869.

Edward A. Preuss sold Francis P. F. Temple a half interest in the ranch and then the two of them deeded their land to a corporation organized for subdivision purposes. The price was $32,000.00.

The name of this corporation was De Las Aguas Land Association, with John P. Schmitz heading its board of trustees and with San Francisco its principal place of business.

Nearly the whole ranch was divided into 75-acre farm lots, with the center reserved for the "Town of Santa Maria," where lots were to be sold for $10.00 each.

1869 Santa Maria

There were 36 blocks in this townsite, with highways running east and west, north and south. The street named "Los Angeles Avenue" is now Wilshire. The others bearing such names as Adelphina, Caroline, Minna and Josephine disappeared along with the German colony.

While the German colony was gasping for life and long after it was dead, two Los Angeles hotel men were buying the land. Parcel by parcel they added to their holdings.

They were Henry Hammel and Andrew H. Denker, managers of the United States Hotel, where "every bed was a spring bed."

They had discovered that the old ranch of Maria Rita Valdez produced good lima beans.

The place became known as the Hammel & Denker Ranch.

A steam train now ran from Los Angeles to Santa Monica through Maria Rita's old home place. Every day it was filled with eager lot-buyers, for the boom of the Eighties was on.

There was a station in Beverly Hills known as Morocco and about the station an entirely imaginary city. It, too, was named Morocco.

Morocco's life was so short the subdivision never reached the County Recorder. It is shown, however, on "V. J. Rowan's Official Map of Los Angeles County (1888)," occupying about the same area as Santa Maria.

To the east of Morocco, and upon the present Hollywood area, the "Townsite of Cahuenga" flowered in 1888, and to the west, in the present Westwood Village site, "Sunset" had an early blooming. The plans for the latter town included the digging of a channel that would bring ocean-going ships up almost to the edge of the Rancho Rodeo de las Aguas.

Soon southern California's boom collapsed and the flowering towns faltered, faded and fell back into the soil from which they sprang.

Deeds from the heirs and successors of Henry Hammel and Andrew H. Denker put the title to what is now Beverly Hills in the Rodeo Land & Water Company. Nearly $670,000.00 passed hands.

This Company had been organized early in 1906 after the oil-drilling ventures of the Amalgamated Oil Company had proved unprofitable.

The new corporation, guided by Burton E. Green, planned a city of homes, with large lots, parks, and streets to be lined with palms, acacias, eucalypti and peppers. Wilbur Cook, a landscape architect from New York, worked out the plans.

The name "Beverly" was chosen after "Beverly Farms," Massachusetts, where Mr. Green had lived.

On November 14, 1906, the subdivision known as "Beverly" was recorded. It was prepared by Daniel S. Halladay, civil engineer. It covered the level land bounded by Wilshire and Santa Monica Boulevards.

On this map appeared for the first time "Beverly," "Rodeo," "Cañon," "Crescent," "Camden," "Roxbury," "Bedford," "Linden," "Burton Way,"—street names known now for the people who live on them.

A few months later, on January 23, 1907, the subdivision of "Beverly Hills" was recorded. It covered the land that sloped up from Santa Monica Boulevard toward the hills. The subdivision was shaped like a giant electric light bulb, with curving streets converging on the northwest.

1906-7
Beverly
Hills

On November 15, 1907, deeds from Rodeo Land & Water Company to Henry C. Clarke were recorded, covering two lots on Crescent Drive, and here Mr. Clarke built Beverly Hills' first house.

The panic of 1907-8 slowed promotion plans. By 1910, however, with Percy H. Clark as general manager of the corporation, lot selling revived and modern Beverly Hills began to take shape.

The year 1912 saw the Beverly Hills Hotel, with

encircling bungalows, rising out of the grain and bean
fields. Margaret J. Anderson, of Hollywood Hotel
fame, was responsible.

When the population reached five hundred, an election was held and the people voted to incorporate,
*1914
Incor-
poration*
naming a temporary board of trustees. Thereupon the
Board of Supervisors declared Beverly Hills a municipal
corporation and filed a copy of its declaration with the
Secretary of State.

In the hills just above the old Rancho boundaries
a new subdivision was laid out. It had high winding
streets that looked down upon Maria Rita's 4500 acres.

On Summit Drive, at the highest point of this subdivision, Douglas Fairbanks bought an estate on April
*1919
Pickfair*
22, 1919, for $35,000.00. It was landscaped, adorned
with an ample dwelling and an encircling wall. It became "Pickfair," the home of Douglas Fairbanks and
Mary Pickford, the social center of the movie colony
and the goal of tourists.

Today busses still stop at 1141 Summit Drive.
Travelers and megaphone wielders look through the
gates toward a white house that rises from the green
forest that has grown at "Pickfair."

This is only one of the many stops on the daily trips
of the sight-seeing busses.

Leaving "Pickfair," the tourist caravan today turns
into San Ysidro Drive, looks through sycamore branches
upon the white brick and the green shutters of the home
of Robert Montgomery. Tower Road to Tower Grove
Drive, a steep hill and John Barrymore's. At the end

of the Road, Miriam Hopkins. Down Benedict Canyon, Carl Laemmle's estate and the vast area that is Harold Lloyd's. On Chevy Chase Drive there is Ralph Morgan and the abode of Charlie Ruggles. Turning into Ridgedale, Frank Morgan on the left and Fredric March and Florence Eldridge on the right.

But this is only a beginning. The busses roll on over smooth curving highways, between lines of immaculate trees, through well kept gardens, on past a hundred other estates of the screen-made people who followed Douglas Fairbanks and Mary Pickford. The megaphone voices echo through the highlands and the lowlands of Beverly Hills.

With vast population movements centering in southern California and with the expanse of the motion picture industry Beverly Hills started to grow.

With the dawn came Charles Chaplin, Gloria Swanson, Fred Niblo and Will Rogers. Then an army of other actors, with producers, writers and studio people, moved in. The Rancho Rodeo de las Aguas burst into a colorful blooming of mansions, villas and homes.

In August of 1923 Will Rogers was writing:

"Lots are sold so quickly and often out here that they are put through escrow made out to the twelfth owner. They couldn't possibly make a separate deed for each purchaser; besides he wouldn't have time to read it the ten minutes time he owned the lot. Your having no money don't worry the agents. If they can just get a couple of dollars down, or an old overcoat or a

1923
Will Rogers
Said . . .

shotgun, or anything to act as first payment. Second hand Fords are considered A-1 collateral."

By 1924 the population was 5000. It had been 500 ten years before.

Between 1922 and 1930 the population of Beverly Hills increased two thousand four hundred and eighty-six per cent.

Today a suave and charming city occupies the plain, the hillsides and the canyons that once belonged to that woman of simple means and simple ways, Maria Rita Valdez.

Today

The land from which this city sprang was first called "Rancho Rodeo de las Aguas," the Ranch of the Gathering of Waters. For a time it was "San Antonio." Then followed "Villa Ranch," "Santa Maria," "Hammel & Denker Ranch," "Morocco" and finally "Beverly Hills." Each name, interpreted, is a chapter in the story of the rise of a well planned, well managed city distinguished for its beauty, wealth and citizens. Today over 30,000 people are grateful for curving tree-lined streets, well groomed parkways, fine schools, ample dwellings, handsome estates, good shops, restaurants and all the evidences of quiet but lustrous living.

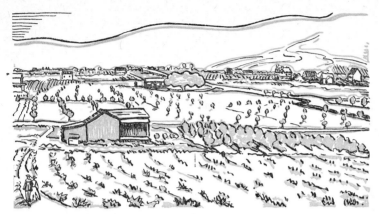

Pasadena from Orange Grove Avenue—1876

PASADENA

and the story of the
RANCHO SAN PASQUAL

THERE WERE several villages of Indians at or near the site of Pasadena when Spanish occupation of California began in 1769.

Indian huts stood on the banks of a brook on the east side of Raymond Hill; at Los Robles Canyon in Oak Knoll; at the mouth of Millard Canyon; and along the Arroyo Seco, especially at the Garfias Springs where today we may look at the same profusion of wild grapes and elderberries, the same sycamores and oaks that were seen by the brown-skinned Gabrielinos. The waters of these springs still gush forth from the bank of the Arroyo at Number 433 Arroyo Boulevard.

The establishment of presidios, missions and pueblos was the aim of the Spanish newcomers.

On the banks of the San Gabriel River near its passage through the southern hills of the valley they started San Gabriel Mission. This was in 1771, ten years before the founding of Los Angeles. A few years later the Mission was moved to its present place at the Indian village of Sibag-na. To the west and northwest lay the live oak forests, the good soil and the streams of the Pasadena, the South Pasadena and the San Marino areas over which the Mission was given jurisdiction. The forests were filled with wild life. Bears abounded in great numbers.

El Rincon de San Pasqual was the name given to the land that was bounded by the Mission of San Gabriel, the mountains and the Arroyo Seco. It included all of the present Pasadena, Altadena, and parts of South Pasadena and San Marino. It was unoccupied except by Indians. It served the interests of San Gabriel as a sheep and cattle ranch. From Millard Canyon an ox-trail led across the Pasadena section to the San Gabriel-Los Angeles road, over which timbers from the mountain forests were hauled into Los Angeles.

Ten or twelve years before California became

Mexican (in 1822), the "Old Mill" had been built, one of the accomplishments of Father Zalvidea. It stands today at 1120 Old Mill Road, a handsome private residence. During Zalvidea's administration, Mission (Wilson) Lake near the mill had been dammed up for irrigation purposes, orchards and vineyards had been planted and fields given over to crops.

Rancho San Rafael, lying west of the Arroyo Seco, had been in the Verdugo family since 1784, in October of which year Governor Fages had given permission to José Maria Verdugo to keep his cattle and horses there upon condition that he do no harm to mission, pueblo or Indians.

Juan Mariné, a native of Catalonia, Spain, obtained a grant of El Rincon de San Pasqual in 1835.

"I, Juan Mariné, a retired lieutenant of artillery of the Department of Mexico, now in Upper California, and a resident of the Mission of San Gabriel, having had the misfortune to lose by the floods of the year 1831 an orchard in the Pueblo of Los Angeles, I went to the Mission of San Gabriel with the Rev. Father Sanchez that he might do me the favor of giving me a parcel of land for cultivation, build a house and keep there my live-stock."

*1833
Juan
Mariné*

With these words Mariné began his petition to Governor Figueroa on July 15, 1833, asking the grant of a rancho. He continued:

"He (Sanchez) informed me that whenever the Indians agreed to it he would be ready.

Whereupon the Indian Alcaldes met and said it was all right and the tract would be given to me. The Rev. Father told them that it would not be for one or two years but forever and they announced that it was all right and they made preparations to measure the lands and give me the place named El Rincon de San Pascual to the cattle where I drove it in the presence of the Sergeant stationed at said Mission, as also the tract where the house is located together with the garden (in the village of San Gabriel) to the extent of one hundred steps in width by three hundred in length."

On the margin of the petition, military fashion, Figueroa wrote:

"Let the Rev. Friar Tomas Estenaga, Minister of this Mission (San Gabriel), make his report hereon."

"There is no obstacle to the grant solicited by the petitioner," replied Estenaga.

The Council, or Ayuntamiento, of the Pueblo of Los Angeles was asked to look into the matter. It found that Mariné had all the qualifications, that he had served his country, "conducting himself honorably," and that the land did not lie "within twenty leagues from the frontiers nor within ten leagues from the littoral." Witnesses were called and their statements were favorable.

So, on February 18, 1835, the Governor gave Mariné a provisional grant and recommended that he

set out fruit or forest trees along his boundaries. In the
Book of Grants at Monterey a record of the transfer
was duly entered.

While all this red tape was being unwound, Mariné
took possession. Being a widower, he had re-married.
His second wife was Eulalia Perez de Guillen, house-
keeper at the Mission, friend and teacher of the Indians.
She was then old, but was destined to long outlive
Mariné and to die at an age so advanced that historians
have been arguing about it ever since.

"When I married him," she once said, "I was
a very old woman, but strong and active, with
scarcely a gray hair. Nevertheless I never had
any children by him."

The celebrated Eulalia is often referred to as the
first owner of San Pasqual. This is technically incorrect,
her husband having that honor. It is possible, however,
that Father Sanchez, who we know played the role
of matchmaker between Eulalia and Mariné and ac-
quiesced in the grant to the husband, was trying to
carry out the obligations of San Gabriel to the old
lady. Eulalia herself considered that Sanchez gave her
the land. She told a story similar to the one outlined
about the Indians raising their right hands to show consent. She added:

"When the land was given me I was already
married to Juan Mariné and afterwards he only
gave me half . . . ."

Juan Mariné died in 1838. His widow retained the
house and garden at San Gabriel and his son, Fruto,

sold his interest in the rancho to José Perez for six horses and ten head of cattle. Perez was the son of a cousin of Eulalia and a favorite violin player at the young people's dances.

The failure of Mariné and of his heirs to cultivate the land or stock it with cattle had thrown the property open, by Mexican law, to acquisition by others. On April 10, 1840, José Perez and Enrique Sepulveda asked for the land, their petition first passing through the hands of Juan Bandini, then administrator of the Mission. (Secularization laws had been enforced at San Gabriel and a civil administration was in charge.) They said the land had been abandoned for the last four years; accordingly, they "denounced" it.

1840
Perez and
Sepulveda

Bandini reported the property to be "vacant sobrantes (surplus lands) for the benefit of the nation," and the Prefect stated that the Mariné heirs had not met the government's requirements.

Accordingly, on September 24, 1840, the Governor granted Rancho San Pasqual to Perez and Sepulveda upon the condition that they would not obstruct the cross-ways and roads and would obey the rules which San Gabriel might adopt as to its "town limits."

The new owners took possession, with their horses and cattle. Each built a small house. If old maps may be relied upon, these rude dwellings were located near the Arroyo Seco (and not in the Adobe Flores region at Raymond Hill).

For the second time El Rincon de San Pasqual was

abandoned by its owners and "denounced" by other
land-seekers.

"I was on the place in the year 1840 or
1841," said Abel Stearns, a witness for the new
applicant, Manuel Garfias. "Sepulveda and Perez
had each a small house on the land which
was occupied. They had stock on the place.
Sepulveda I recollect had a pretty good stock of
horses and mares and a small stock of cattle.
Perez I think had stock there. The occupation
of Perez continued until he died, which was, I
think, in 1841. Sepulveda I think occupied it
until his death which was I believe in 1843 . . ."

At Perez' death his cattle and horses were sent to
the ranch of Antonio Maria Lugo, the widow's father.
Sepulveda's animals were killed, stolen or scattered,
"all of which," he explained, "made me give up the
desire to stock and cultivate the place."

Garfias, a young officer in the Mexican army, paid
$70.00 to Sepulveda and $100.00 to the widow of
Perez to compensate them for the two adobe houses.

*1843
Garfias of
the Army*

On November 28, 1843, he received the formal
grant from the Governor and took possession.

A year before the signing of the Treaty by which
California was ceded to the United States, the Pasadena
area figured in the contest between American troops
and Mexican.

After being defeated at the Battle of Mesa (January
9, 1847), the Californians under General Flores with-

drew to the Rancho San Pasqual and to the south slope
of Raymond Hill. Here were a stream of water, an oak
grove and a building (now "Adobe Flores"). Sentinel
horsemen were posted on top of Raymond Hill to
watch for the coming of the United States troops. The
Americans, however, ignored them; instead of march-
ing to Pasadena they went into Los Angeles with flags
flying and took formal possession.

When the three members of the Board of Land
Commissioners, Felch, Campbell and Thompson, arrived in Los Angeles in August of 1852, they were
greeted most warmly, especially by those who expected
to file land claims. Manuel Garfias gave a grand ball in
their honor at his Main and First Street adobe residence
in Los Angeles. The Commission had been created by
the federal government the year after California was
admitted as a state to the Union in 1850.

*1852
Grand
Ball*

When Garfias filed his claim to San Pasqual on
September 16, 1852, he accompanied it with a wealth
of evidence and followed this up with the depositions
of such eminent southlanders as Pio Pico, José Antonio
Carrillo, Manuel Dominguez, Antonio F. Coronel,
Ygnacio del Valle, Fernando Sepulveda, Augustin Olvera, Abel Stearns and José del Carmen Lugo.

The claim was approved in 1854, Thompson de-
livering the opinion. It was not until April 3, 1863,
however, that the United States patent was issued.
Abraham Lincoln's signature appeared on this document. The survey, when completed, included more
than thirteen thousand five hundred acres in the rancho.

Meanwhile Garfias built an adobe house not far
from the springs where the Indians once had a village.
It became famous as a country place, a favorite spot
for Los Angeles friends of the owner. Judge Benjamin
S. Eaton, coming to San Pasqual Rancho in 1858, visited
at the "Garfias hacienda." He described it as one of
the finest country establishments in southern California.

*1858
Judge
Eaton*

> "It was a one and a half story adobe building,
> with walls two feet thick, all nicely plastered in-
> side and out, and had an ample corridor extend-
> ing all around. It had board floors, and boasted
> of green blinds—a rare thing in those days. This
> structure cost $5,000.00—in fact, it cost Garfias
> his ranch, for he had to borrow money to build
> it."

The walls of the Garfias adobe were pulled down
during the boom of the Eighties to make way for a
subdivision. The land on which the house stood is now
owned by Charles Gibbs Adams. The ancient oak tree
which it faced still grows near the edge of the arroyo.
Known today as Cathedral Oak, it has inspired pleasant
legends about Spanish explorers and Easter services in
1770, legends that are not borne out by known fact.

San Pasqual was not the best of cattle ranges and
when dry years came the fortunes of Manuel Garfias
suffered. Then, too, Garfias liked politics better than
ranching; he liked it better than serving in the army
under Flores. While he acted as the county treasurer
of Los Angeles in 1850-51, his mother-in-law, Doña
Encarnacion Sepulveda de Abila, ran the ranch. Finally

his borrowings, at the usual ruinous rates of interest, forced him to sacrifice his property.

*1859-60
Wilson and
Griffin*
In January of 1859 Garfias deeded the ranch to Benjamin D. Wilson, the disclosed consideration being $1,800.00. The following year, in May, Wilson gave John S. Griffin—Doctor Griffin—a half interest for $4,000.00.

Benjamin D. Wilson—Don Benito—after whom a mountain, a canyon, a lake, a ditch, a trail, an avenue and a school were named, had come to Los Angeles with trappers in 1841. In 1852 he bought what was known as the Lake Vineyard property, adjoining San Pasqual, where he built his home near the "Old Mill." Dr. John S. Griffin had come as Chief Medical Officer with the American Army.

In 1867, Wilson and Griffin, with the aid of Eaton, built the Wilson Ditch, the first attempt to lead the waters of the Arroyo Seco from Devil's Gate up to the mesa land of San Pasqual.

From time to time various parts of the ranch were sold and in 1873 Wilson and Griffin partitioned the unsold portion between them. Griffin, who wished to sell out to the "Indiana Colony," took approximately four thousand acres. Wilson, who wanted to hold on, took sixteen hundred acres. The Griffin land included the original site of Pasadena.

One fall day in 1873, Judge Eaton took a visitor from Indiana to the San Pasqual Ranch. They drove from Los Angeles, following the Arroyo Seco, stopping at the Garfias adobe and then on to "Fair Oaks,"

Eaton's home.   The pleasant valley and the luminous mountains captivated the Judge's guest, who was D. M. Berry, purchasing agent for the "California Colony of Indiana." This organization of Indiana people, hopeful of emigrating to California, had grown out of a meeting of friends at Dr. T. B. Elliott's home in Indianapolis one cold Sunday during the winter of 1872-73.   Berry had been sent on to spy out the promised land.

When at last Berry saw the San Pasqual Ranch, after weary months of colony-site hunting, he knew he need go no further.   Meanwhile the panic of 1873 had nearly wrecked his original Indiana group.   So, to buy and colonize San Pasqual land, he formed a new organization in Los Angeles, the "San Gabriel Orange Grove Association," most of the stockholders of which were not Hoosiers.   Before the end of the year incorporation was completed.   Capital stock in the amount of $25,-000.00, divided into shares of $250.00 each, was subscribed for by those eager to settle on the rancho.

*1873
Colony
Plans*

On December 26, 1873, John S. Griffin made a deed of his four thousand acres to Thomas F. Croft, one of the directors of the new corporation, and three days later Croft gave title to the San Gabriel Orange Grove Association.   The consideration passing to Griffin was $25,000.00.

By ten in the morning of January 27, 1874, buggies began to arrive on the plain that was to be Pasadena. In the buggies were men, women, children and picnic baskets.   The hills were green and flowers were out, for there had been early rains.

Since buying Griffin's land, the San Gabriel Orange Grove Association had surveyed and platted fifteen hundred acres lying west of what is now Fair Oaks Avenue, each colonist to get fifteen acres for each share of stock. (Two years more were to pass before B. D. Wilson's holdings, lying east of the Avenue, would be subdivided.) The lots ranged on both sides of Orange Grove Avenue, which was given its name by Calvin Fletcher.

1874
A City
Begins

After lunch, on that important January day in 1874, there was a roll call of colonists. Then the lots were chosen and assigned.

Cultivation began at once. By the end of May the colony had houses, a reservoir to hold 3,000,000 gallons of water, an irrigating system, eighty acres of grain raised for hay, 100,000 grape cuttings set out, 10,000 small trees purchased for nursery planting and a large area of land prepared for corn.

Apparently no colonist had thought of drawing upon local terms in christening the village. So "Indiana Colony" gave way to "Pasadena" at a meeting of the San Gabriel Orange Grove Association held April 22, 1875. "Pasadena," coined out of the Chippewa language, was offered by Dr. T. B. Elliott. It is usually translated "Crown of the Valley."

Pasadena began on Orange Grove Avenue in 1874. That avenue today is one of the stately boulevards of the world. Pasadena itself has pushed toward the old borders of "El Rincon de San Pasqual." The San

Today

Gabriel Mountains, as lovely as in mission and rancho days, form a magic boundary for a city and region whose spreading oaks, many gardens and pleasant homes have charmed visitors ever since the Raymond opened its doors in 1886 as the first "tourist hotel." Pasadena through the years has made many acquisitions, so many in fact that the name itself suggests: Tournament of Roses; football on New Year's Day in the Rose Bowl; California Institute of Technology and Doctor Millikan; the Huntington Library (just over the border in San Marino); Mount Wilson and a telescope that pushes back the limits of space; imposing churches on Colorado Street; a Civic Center with long vistas and dignified buildings; a Community Playhouse of distinguished achievement; leisurely living; and such neighbors as Altadena, South Pasadena and San Marino. The eighty-five thousand people who now live in Pasadena have made of Juan Mariné's rancho a famous and beautiful city.

Monrovia, After An Early Print

MONROVIA

and the story of the
RANCHO SANTA ANITA
and the
RANCHO AZUSA DE DUARTE

WHEN SPANIARDS began their occupation of California in 1769 the site of Monrovia was a woodland of ancient oaks sloping up to high mountains. It overlooked, and was a part of, a valley that is the San Gabriel.

186

The nearest Indian village was Asuksa-gna, which gave its name to the present city of Azusa. A hunter from this village, entering the Monrovia woodland, would have heard only the whirring wings of quail, the voices of birds and the movement of small animal life in the brush.

1769
Woodland
of Oaks

On the banks of the San Gabriel River, where it passed through the southern hills of the valley, was the San Gabriel Mission's first location. A few years later it moved to its present place.

The whole valley, including the Monrovia region, came under the jurisdiction of the Mission. For many years thereafter the story of the San Gabriel Valley is the story of Monrovia.

When California turned from Spain to Mexico in 1822 the oak-covered, boulder-strewn upland of Monrovia still lay untouched by man, a paradise for lizards and squirrels. Not far away, however, under the direction of the Franciscan fathers at San Gabriel, the lower portions of the valley were being used for stock-raising and the cultivation of grapes and grain. Indians, Mission-trained, tended great herds of cattle, horses and sheep, tilled the fields and looked after orange, apple and fig orchards.

Toward the southwest the valley road led from the Mission to the Pueblo of Los Angeles, forty-one years old, a farming center, with vineyards, cornfields and squat adobe houses. To the northeast the road extended from the Mission toward the Cucamonga and San Bernardino regions.

Early in January of 1836 a petition was laid before the Ayuntamiento or Council of Los Angeles. It read:

"Very Illustrious Council: I, Hugo Reid, native of Great Britain . . . represent that for two years I have resided in this territory and eight in this country, unmarried, and finding myself with the intention of settling in this city . . . I pray your honors that you consider me as having appeared and please to issue to me a testimony of this representation and of whatever you may consider proper to decree."

When citizenship was given him, Reid looked about for a wife. He married Victoria, an Indian woman at the Mission who had been trained by Doña Eulalia Perez.

Having obtained citizenship and a wife, Reid wanted land. East of San Gabriel was a vast oak-covered area known since early days as Santa Anita. The minutes of the Los Angeles Council described it in 1839 as a "place occupied by a small number of sheep and goats of the Mission of San Gabriel, to which it belongs, and some cornfields of some Indians of said establishment." It extended almost to what is now Azusa and on the north pressed up against the blue wall of the San Gabriel Mountains, sometimes called Sierra Madre. Within its boundaries lay most of Monrovia's site.

Reid was eager to acquire Santa Anita. Several other citizens also wanted it, among them Bernardino Lopez, José Antonio Carrillo and José Antonio Yorba.

Reid asked for Santa Anita in 1839 and in due time got it.

"I have a better right," he said, ". . . being married to the daughter of the Mission . . . who worked personally, both she and her parents and her former husband, in the foundation of the establishment."

It was easy to get good land when secularization at San Gabriel was completed and the Mission's activities were curtailed.

Governor Alvarado on April 16, 1841, gave Hugo Reid provisional title to Rancho Santa Anita. On behalf of the Mission, Fray Tomas Estenaga expressed his approval, describing the grant to Reid as "a reward for services rendered for the benefit of this Mission by his wife and her late husband Pablo, who did greatly contribute to the existence of the said Mission."

1841 Two Grants

On May 10, 1841, the Governor made another grant, to the chagrin of Reid, who felt he was being despoiled. This conveyance was to Citizen Andrés Duarte of land known as the Azusa.

A dispute at once arose as to the location of the dividing line between the Santa Anita and the Azusa Ranchos. Ygnacio Palomares acted as peacemaker and persuaded Reid and Duarte to accept a line drawn from a certain "oak tree lying to the west of Azusa on which tree there were made some blazes." Today the dividing line is identified by Norumbega Drive extending southwesterly from Sawpit Wash. Monrovia boundaries take in part of both ranchos.

In 1843 Reid's provisional title was renewed by Governor Micheltorena. Finally on March 31, 1845, Governor Pio Pico granted him a title in fee simple to three square leagues of grazing land, bounded on the east by Azusa de Duarte and on the west by Rancho San Pasqual. Reid was placed officially in possession of Santa Anita and, to make his title unimpeachable, Pico's grant was approved by the Departmental Assembly.

In May of 1847, Reid sold his Rancho Santa Anita, and with it the home he had built on what is now Baldwin Lake. For himself he retained land and "a new house" near the Mission.

By the formal language of the Mexican deed of conveyance, Don Perfecto Hugo Reid declared that the selling price of $2700.00 was a "just price" and the "true value" of the ranch and that he could not find "anyone who would offer more."

*1847
Dalton:
Ranchero*

The buyer was Henry Dalton, sometimes addressed as Don Enrique Dalton. He was an Englishman who had been a merchant in Peru for twenty-five years. He came to California in 1843 with the ambition to become a ranchero.

Miners, drifting down from the Gold Rush country soon after California became a state, in 1850, found their way into the pleasant streams of the San Gabriel Valley. They worked back into the Sawpit and Santa Anita Canyons. Until 1870 the foothills about Monrovia rang with the voices and sounds of men carrying picks, shovels and pans.

Small quantities of gold were obtained. No one became rich.

Henry Dalton, who had a Mexican title, went before the Board of Land Commissioners to have this title confirmed by the United States. He petitioned for Santa Anita on September 14, 1852. Andrés Duarte petitioned for Azusa on October 6, 1853. They submitted lengthy proofs of title and curious *diseños*, or maps, dating from Mexican days.

Both claims were approved by the Board and its decisions were upheld on appeal to the District Court.

Patents from the United States were issued to the claimants, one during the presidency of Andrew Johnson, and the other in Rutherford B. Hayes' administration. Long before the patents came from Washington new owners were in possession of both ranches.

The early Sixties were years of fearful drought in southern California. Great ranchos were broken up as a result, and many were lost to their Spanish-speaking owners through foreclosure.

The San Gabriel Valley lay white with the bones of cattle. The thirty-day flood that ended the drought brought destruction to surviving cattle.

William Wolfskill, pioneer orange grower, held a mortgage on Andrés Duarte's land. He foreclosed it and at the sheriff's sale his own bid of $4000.00 for the sixty-five hundred-acre Azusa de Duarte was the highest.

At about the same time Wolfskill also acquired the Santa Anita ranch. Dalton's ownership of it had lasted seven years. Then Joseph A. Rowe, the circus man,

1864-5
William
Wolfskill

had bought it for $33,000.00. It would make good winter quarters for lions, tigers and elephants. Failure of such plans put the title to the three square leagues of land in William Corbitt and Albert Diblee, who in turn conveyed to Wolfskill at the close of the Civil War.

Thus all of Monrovia came into one man's hands.

One day in 1874, Lucky Baldwin, the mining king, made a trip through the San Gabriel Valley to look at some property in the San Bernardino Mountains. He had come from San Francisco.

The rich soil, the rolling contours, the forest of oaks and the high blue wall of the Sierra Madre left a lasting picture in his mind.

The following year, after another visit to Los Angeles and the San Gabriel Valley, he went to the office of Harris Newmark, prominent merchant and owner of Santa Anita. Newmark had bought Wolfskill's Santa Anita in 1872 for $85,000.00.

Baldwin carried a tin box under his arm. He was prepared to pay $150,000.00 cash for Santa Anita. Newmark played his best cards and Lucky was soon glad to meet the price of $200,000.00. The box was opened and $12,500.00 in currency was counted out.

"That will bind the sale," Baldwin said, "until I can examine the title."

A few days later the balance was paid. A deed to Elias J. Baldwin was issued on April 8, 1875, conveying more than eight thousand acres. Water rights and personal property went with the acreage, except that New-

1875
Lucky
Baldwin

mark held back three mules, seven cows, six calves, one bull and a hundred cords of cut wood.

Lucky Baldwin immediately invested $100,000.00 in Kentucky thoroughbreds. He built racing stables. Near the present Arcadia he erected a club house.

He got together with his neighbors, after several years of dispute, and improved the irrigating system that brought water for Azusa de Duarte and Santa Anita from the canyons back of Monrovia. He substituted a tile pipe flume for the dirt ditch.

Baldwin did not own Azusa de Duarte. It had been sold in 1868 by Lewis Wolfskill, son of William, to Alexander Weill, a New York capitalist. Weill and Wolfskill had taken the first steps to develop water for the mutual benefit of the ranches.

In due time Lucky Baldwin got the fever to sub-divide and sell. All that portion of his ranch that lay east of his home place he cut up into acreage lots. His subdivision extended east from Santa Anita Avenue and north and south of White Oak Avenue, now Foothill Boulevard. It included most of the Monrovia area.

This was in 1883. Two years later the map of the subdivision was recorded at the request of Monrovia's first settler: William N. Monroe.

In April of 1884 William N. Monroe came to south-ern California—not to found a city but to settle down. He had been a Civil War cavalry scout, an Indian fighter and for many years a railroad builder. His work had taken him over the whole of the West and into

Mexico. Now, with $150,000.00 saved up, he was ready for a permanent home.

To see the country about Los Angeles he bought a spring wagon and a pair of ponies.

One morning Mr. and Mrs. Monroe drove out into the San Gabriel Valley. They stopped at Lucky Baldwin's club house.

"Let me show you some land," Lucky told them.

*1884
Monroe's
Ride*

Behind fast horses Baldwin took the Monroes for a drive over his vast ranch. They sped through the meadow-land of magnificent oaks and to the valley uplands. High loomed the Sierra Madre, every ridge lined in blue mist.

Baldwin and his guests neared the eastern boundary of the new subdivision. South of what is now Colorado Boulevard extended a barley field. North lay a woodland of ancient oaks sloping up to the base of the mountains.

Pointing toward the Santa Anita and Sawpit Canyons, Baldwin said:

"They will supply you with water and they will protect you against frost."

Driving north the party stopped at what is now the intersection of Primrose and Oaks Avenues. Giant oaks gave shade. Mr. and Mrs. Monroe were delighted, so much so that later they chose the same spot as a building site for their home, "The Oaks."

That night the Monroes stayed at Baldwin's club house and the next day they took a second excursion to the upland that was to be Monrovia. This settled the matter for them and the purchase of several thirty-acre parcels was arranged.

In the course of a few months a deed was to be issued to W. N. Monroe for 120 acres lying on both sides of White Oak Avenue (Foothill Boulevard). It showed a consideration of $15,000.00 paid Baldwin. In March of 1885 a deed for 90 acres more would be delivered at a price of $11,105.00 and a third deed of 30 acres at $3750.00, this last to be in favor of C. O. Monroe, brother of W. N. Monroe.

In May of 1884, one month after their trip with Lucky Baldwin, the Monroes had pitched a tent under the oaks that still stand at the southeast corner of Hillcrest and Magnolia in Monrovia. Close by were the red foothills and beyond them the mountains.

From the camp Monroe directed a large force of Chinamen and mules.

"Clear the land of boulders and brush," were his orders, "but leave the oaks."

Water was brought upon the land from the canyons of Sawpit and Santa Anita. Pepper trees were planted.

A cottage was built, to be used until "The Oaks" could be finished: that comfortable frame mansion that still stands beneath ancient shade near Primrose and Oaks Avenues and that was to be long a gathering place for the townspeople of Monrovia and its visitors.

In the cottage the first school was held as soon as Monroe could organize a school district. Fifteen children were required. He himself had four to contribute toward this minimum number. His brother had three, and two families living near the San Gabriel River furnished five. Three more children were needed. W. N. Monroe, ever resourceful, went over to Baldwin's ranch and borrowed a family that exactly supplied the want.

To found a town, W. N. Monroe joined hands with Judge J. D. Bicknell, Los Angeles attorney, E. F. Spence, banker, and J. F. Crank, railroad man.

1886
Birth of
Monrovia

All had bought Santa Anita acreage of E. J. Baldwin. In addition, Spence and Bicknell had secured a portion of the Azusa de Duarte that had belonged to Alexander Weill (and his successors, L. L. Bradbury, James Craig and V. E. Howard).

In March of 1886 engineers laid out the townsite of Monrovia. It centered about Myrtle and Orange Avenues, Orange now being Colorado Boulevard. The streets were given the names of trees, flowers and girls. Myrtle Avenue, the principal business street, was named after Myrtle Monroe, daughter of the first settler.

On May 17, 1886, the townsite was opened to lot buyers who came from Duarte, San Gabriel and Los Angeles.

On that day, with a throng of buggies and wagons parked beneath the oaks, and an auctioneer accepting bids of $100.00 for inside lots and $150.00 for corner lots, Monrovia began.

The opening-day sales were many. They kept up

on days following, aided by the great real estate boom that was sweeping southern California.

The new town was ready to call itself a city when on November 7, 1887, it filed a petition for incorporation with the Board of Supervisors of Los Angeles County. It not only had five hundred people but also it had a Grand View Hotel; an Odd Fellows' Lodge; a post office; a Pioneer Livery and Feed Stable; a carpenters' union; a two-story school with a central tower; Barnes' general store with town hall above; Davis and Rush's butcher shop; a Women's Christian Temperance Union; Miss Killian's Millinery Shop; an Emporium of Fashion; a First National Bank; a Methodist Church holding three hundred and fifty people; a five-thousand-dollar Baptist Church; milk delivery by horseback; Lawrence's Hardware Store; and mule cars running up Myrtle Avenue.

Today, Monrovia, from its front porch, looks out over the San Gabriel Valley patterned with towns, orange groves and long boulevards, the same valley that once was drowsy with the life of California's pastoral age.

Today

Today, Monrovia, stepping to its back porch, looks up to age-old mountains with their changing colors, shadows and flowing mists.

Monrovia's setting is a woodland of native oaks. Among them have grown pepper, magnolia, acacia, persimmon, avocado and citrus trees. Here are the homes of fifteen thousand people. White-walled, red-roofed, they are set in gardens on deeply shaded streets. Here, also, are public parks and a lively business section.

Good crops and pleasant living spring from the upland that was selected and settled by William N. Monroe.

Harvest of The Valley

POMONA

and the story of the
RANCHO SAN JOSÉ

SPANISH OCCUPATION of California in 1769 was begun by the "leather-jackets" who marched north from Loreto to San Diego with Captain Rivera. It was followed by the gradual establishment of presidios, missions and pueblos.

The Pomona Valley, shaped like a fruit basket, lay then, as now, in the arms of curving, oak-dotted hills. On the north loomed the higher San Gabriels and snow-capped Mt. San Antonio.

In the valley plain, in 1769, were several ciénegas or swamps, two or three ribbons of green made by the willows and sycamores that lined creeks and washes, and here and there groups of crouching live oaks. Away from the water sources the landscape took on the olive color of the native grasses and of the chaparral: a scattering of wild buckwheat, button-sage, wild mahogany, scrub-oak, pigeon berry and prickly-pear cactus.

*1769
Indians*

The Indian population of the valley was small and probably migratory, keeping to the places where water was available.

There was an Indian settlement at the large spring near what is now the intersection of Town and San Bernardino Avenues in Pomona. The exact location is shown on the recorded survey made in 1874 of the land purchased by A. R. Meserve and C. F. Loop.

Ganesha Park also, favored now by picnickers, was once favored by Indians.

Another Indian site was Indian Hill, a mesa lying north of the present Claremont and reached by following the extension of College Way beyond its intersection with Foothill Boulevard. This mesa, commanding a view of the lowland valley, is today devoted to golf-playing, but it was long the scene of Indian activities and festivities. The first white settler in the Claremont region, W. T. Martin, arriving in the winter of 1870-71, found forty-five brush huts and two hundred Indians living among the oaks at the southeast corner of the mesa. Not until 1883 did the last of them leave.

Another old Indian camping place was Mud Springs, a natural water source surrounded by a marsh, located about a mile southeast of the present town of San Dimas, and just east of where the Santa Fe Railroad crosses Artesia Street. It lay on an ancient trail. The Anza party, on its path-finding march north from Sonora, Mexico, in 1774, and Jedediah Smith, the first white man to reach California overland from the eastern United States, in 1826, are thought to have passed through Mud Springs.

When California became Mexican territory in 1822 the site of Pomona and the Pomona Valley were still unoccupied by white people.

Sheep from the Mission of San Gabriel, guided by Indian herders, grazed over the curving hills, when they were green with pasturage, and along the water courses. The valley itself was claimed by the Mission and had been under its jurisdiction since its establishment in 1771.

1822
Sheep of
San Gabriel

Priests from San Gabriel and citizens from the pueblo of Los Angeles, founded ten years after the Mission, occasionally rode through the valley area. A trail or road led northeast toward Cucamonga, where there was an Indian rancheria, and toward the San Bernardino area, a good cattle country for the Mission.

Not until 1837 did white men settle in Pomona Valley, then called San José after the stream of that name.

On March 27, 1837, a petition was placed in the hands of the Governor of California. It came from two Los Angeles citizens: Ygnacio Palomares and Ricardo Vejar.

"We have a considerable number of cattle and horses," the petitioners said, "being our only means for the support of our families . . . which are now upon a place very small and inconvenient, where they do not thrive . . . and the place being vacant which is known by the name of San José, distant some six leagues, more or less, from the Ex-Mission of San Gabriel, a map of which place we will lay before your Excellency as soon as possible—we respectfully ask you to grant us the said place, considering the smallness of the place in which we now are, for which cause it is that we appeal to your Excellency's goodness . . . praying that you will receive this on common paper there being none of the proper seal . . . For myself and for Ricardo Vejar who does not know how to write. (Signed) Ygn. Palomares."

1837
Two
Petitioners

Palomares, the petitioner, was the son of Cristobal Palomares who had gone from Mexico, as a soldier, to Monterey. From Monterey, Cristobal had moved to Santa Barbara and later to Los Angeles, where he died leaving sons and daughters.

Ricardo Vejar, born in San Diego, was an old-time friend of the Palomares family. He was the son of Salvador Vejar, who had come to California via Mexico. Ricardo had been living on the Rancho Rodeo de las Aguas (the present Beverly Hills).

Governor Alvarado turned the land plea over to the Los Angeles Ayuntamiento or City Council for investigation. This was the usual procedure, Los Angeles having had jurisdiction in such matters for several years, ever since secularization at San Gabriel had been completed.

The Council's Committee on Vacant Lands looked into the request of Palomares and Vejar and reported:

"The parties interested . . . are Mexican citizens by birth, have rendered repeated services to this jurisdiction and have a considerable stock of cattle and horses . . . which stock is at present on a piece of land given to them temporarily, in common with the residents of this city, which is small and on which there is a scarcity of water and pasture. The place San José . . . is now vacant . . . Although it has belonged to the Ex-Mission of San Gabriel . . . there is not upon it a single head of cattle belonging to this Community. Wherefore the Committee thinks that it is in a condition to be granted in conformity to the laws of colonization."

Back to Alvarado at Santa Barbara went the petition with its attached documents. The Governor on April 15, 1837, wrote:

". . . The Citizens Ygnacio Palomares and Ricardo Vejar are declared owners in property of the place called San José . . . Let the proper decree be issued and recorded in the proper book . . ."

On the same day he executed a formal deed, "in the name of the Mexican nation," and four days later the state legislative body confirmed the grant.

There was one more formal step to be taken to give the new owners a perfect Mexican title. That was for them to be placed officially in possession, a duty that fell upon the alcalde, or mayor, of Los Angeles.

Accordingly, on August 3, 1837, José Sepulveda, the alcalde, accompanied by two chain bearers and a surveyor, proceeded horseback to the southeasterly corner of the rancho of San José, among the hills called the "lomas of Santa Ana." They had a cord one hundred varas long and to each end was attached a wooden stake. They took a black willow tree as a starting point and between its limbs they placed a dry stick in the form of a cross. Thence they proceeded westerly toward the Puente Hills, continuing northerly, easterly and southerly around the whole of San José. Proper landmarks were placed as they went.

No sooner had judicial possession been given them than Palomares and Vejar took actual possession. Accompanied by their families, their vaqueros, their cattle, their sheep and all their goods, they moved into the fertile San José. By its streams they built homes and corrals and planted corn, potatoes, beans and peppers.

*1837
Possession*

Señor Vejar chose a homesite on the Arroyo Pedregoso, the waters of which flowed westerly to join those of San José Creek. Close by the southern hills he built an adobe house. Long since gone, it stood east of the spot, in Spadra, where the brick mansion of Louis Phillips was later to rise and a few feet north of the present Pomona Sewage Disposal Plant. Until 1844 this was to be Ricardo's home.

Señor Palomares built a home, too, not far from present Ganesha Park and between Preciado and Walnut Streets. Its exact location has been questioned. The pleasant old ranch house that still stands buried in trees and vines at No. 1569 North Park Avenue is that very home, according to Don Ygnacio's grandson, F. J. Palomares, who lived there prior to 1882.

> "It was the first habitation built in Pomona," he said, in a letter of August 14, 1936. "I believe that the house at some time or another was somewhat larger . . . I faintly remember some adobes and the ruins of some in the rear portion of the house, and it may have been that some of them were used either in adding rooms or in repair work."

The two pioneer families had no sooner become well settled than Palomares' brother-in-law, Luis Arenas, asked to share with the other two in the San José. An additional league of land—to become known in part as the San José Addition—was obtained from Governor Alvarado, who thereupon regranted the enlarged ranch to the three partners: Palomares, Vejar, Arenas. That was on March 14, 1840.

1840 Expansion

Arenas chose for himself a location on the old San Bernardino road near the present corner of Gibbs and McKinley Avenues. Nearby was a large spring. For many years thereafter freight teams on their way to

San Bernardino stopped at Arenas' place for water.

Ramon Vejar, son of Ricardo, later reminiscing of this pioneering period, said:

"The San José was a cattle ranch. When we killed, there would be two hundred head killed at a time. The tallow was melted into bags of skins and the beef was dried . . . We milked forty cows and made cheese and butter."

Owning land in undivided shares did not work out well in the San José Rancho and in 1845 Ricardo Vejar and Henry Dalton (who had bought out Luis Arenas) were asking for a partition. They went before Juan Gallardo with their request, Gallardo being "Judge of the First Instance and First Alcalde of Los Angeles."

"We pray you to do as we request," they petitioned, "subjecting ourselves to the payment of the dues which of right are chargeable to each of us."

Palomares, too, said he favored partition, being curious to know what he owned. But he informed the Judge he had no intention of paying any part of the partition expenses, for already he had paid more than his share in getting the ranch.

Judge Gallardo went ahead with the partition, dispatching a surveyor, Don Gaspar Farrell, and chain bearers to the Pomona scene. For five days, in February of 1846, they toiled over the rolling hills and broad valley of the Rancho San José. On the sixth day they produced a map and—for Mexican days—a very good

1846 Survey, Partition

one. To it Judge Gallardo gave his approval on February 12, 1846.

By the partition the whole southerly portion of the Rancho went to Vejar, the greater part of the northerly portion to Palomares and the extreme northwesterly portion to Dalton.

The original townsite of Pomona was to fall within the boundaries of the Vejar allotment, and all of the present Pomona is within the Vejar and the Palomares boundaries.

This partition was the cause of later disputes, but time, quit claim deeds, quiet title actions, foreclosures and deaths finally smoothed out all the title difficulties.

The Pomona Valley had been little disturbed by the Mexican War, though echoes of the conflict were heard from the so-called Battle of Chino, a skirmish fought on Isaac Williams' Rancho Santa Ana del Chino adjoining San José on the southeast. Life flowed on as usual even when California was ceded to the United States by the Treaty of Guadalupe Hidalgo in 1848.

1848
A
Treaty

The current problems of Rancho San José continued to be water and Indians. A seven-mile ditch was dug, bringing water from the San Antonio Canyon to supplement that obtainable from the Palomares Ciénega, and the various springs and the San José Creek were drawn upon heavily to take care of the irrigation and domestic needs of the Palomares and Vejar establishments and of a few other families that had come into the valley.

The Indians of the region worked for the whites but those from the mountains and deserts now and then made cattle raids. Ricardo Vejar, possibly because of the Indian menace, in 1844 had abandoned the old homestead on the Arroyo Pedregoso and moved to what is now Walnut. There he built a large walled adobe, secure from attack, and there he was to remain until his death in 1882. On the Walnut site today is the home of E. R. Forster, commanding a thrilling view of valley and hills. Vejar's sons, Ramon and Francisco (Chico), built other houses in the Spadra region.

California was admitted as a state to the Union in 1850 and the next year the Board of Land Commissioners was created to investigate and pass upon land titles in California.

Ygnacio Palomares and Ricardo Vejar petitioned for approval of their title in September and October of 1852. They based their claim on Mexican grants, the two from Governor Alvarado, including the original *1852* one made on April 15, 1837, the re-grant on March *Before* 14, 1840, which included the additional league, and a *the Board* third from Governor (pro tem) Manuel Jimeno in favor of Arenas for still another league of grazing land made on November 8, 1841.

The Board approved the claims and recognized the partition of 1846.

Not until January 20, 1875, however, during Grant's administration, did the United States issue its patent to Ygnacio Palomares, Ricardo Vejar and Henry

Dalton. The government survey and patent showed over twenty-two thousand acres.

Waiting upon commissioners and district court officials, however, did not interfere with life in and near the valley of San José. Judge Benjamin Hayes, who electioneered through the section in the fifties and sixties and once spent $400 on a ball he gave for prospective voters, wrote in his diary that the place was "full of agreeable people, fond of festivity, industrious withal." He sat down to a family dinner, on one occasion, probably at Ricardo's Walnut house, where the feasters numbered a hundred, all members of the Vejar establishments.

The finest adobe house in the whole region, though not the largest, was the Ramon Vejar place. A two-story building dating from 1855, it still stands on the Diamond Bar Ranch property near Spadra, its upper veranda looking out over the valley and to the high blue peaks of the San Gabriels.

The famous Butterfield Stage, beginning operations in 1858, passed through a portion of the San José ranch, carrying passengers from San Francisco to St. Louis, Missouri. Leaving the ranch it followed the Chino road southeasterly.

The old records of Los Angeles County disclose a deed of the Rancho San José made on April 30, 1864, by Ricardo Vejar. It was in favor of Isaac Schlesinger and Hyman Tischler. The consideration shown was $28,000.00.

*1864
Vejar
Loses*

Back of that document, which people today would call a "deed in lieu of foreclosure," was the dispersal of a patriarchal family and a bitterness that swept the whole Pomona Valley.

Vejar, like most of the early California ranch owners, borrowed money during the terrible drought years of the Sixties. The money came from shrewd American merchants. It was lent at interest rates, then legal, that sent the original debt skyrocketing.

Neither Schlesinger nor Tischler, the new owners, dared to enjoy their ranch.

One day an attempt was made to waylay Tischler on his way through the valley, but the wrong man was shot. Soon afterward Tischler disappeared. Some say he was ambushed and killed while on a trip to San Bernardino, others that he got away to San Francisco.

In April of 1864 Ygnacio Palomares dictated his will.

"In the name of God and of the Great Creator, considering that we are all mortals and being a little ill, I wish to dispose of the small fortune that God has given me, before being deprived of the corporeal faculties with which the nature of man is endowed . . . I charge that when my soul is parted from my body, this shall be buried in the graveyard where part of my family is already laid . . . My burial shall be simple and without pomp . . . I leave my wife absolute owner of . . . the land of the Rancho, excepting the portions my sons possess . . ."

Ygnacio died in November following.

Soon after Schlesinger and Tischler acquired the Vejar property they looked about for a man to run the place, since life there was too dangerous for them.

A prudent young German, with the French name of Louis Phillips, was living in Paredon Blanco, now Boyle Heights, Los Angeles. Tischler went to him.

"Take charge of our ranch at San José," he told Phillips, "and we'll pay you $100 a month and half of the increase in sheep, calves and colts."

Louis Phillips accepted and took immediate and successful charge.

Before the two owners disappeared from the Pomona scene they gave Phillips a quit claim deed for the ranch. It was dated April 6, 1866. The consideration was said to be $30,000.00.

1866
Louis
Phillips

Louis Phillips made San José prosper. He avoided debt and cultivated the good will of his neighbors and of his workers. He bought more cattle and sheep and over the fertile plain on which a city was to rise he sent his herds to browse on rich alfilaria and wild oats. From his two-story brick house, still standing on Valley Boulevard in Spadra and called the Cecil George place, he ran a ranch and a store.

Meanwhile Americans were drifting into the valley, some coming from the "Willow Grove" and "Lexington" settlements on the San Gabriel River. These settlements, which soon became one under the name of El Monte (meaning thicket), had been started in the early fifties by pioneers from Salt Lake City and from places east who had taken the trail that led into the San Bernardino Valley.

One of the newcomers to San José from El Monte was William Rubottom, known as Uncle Billy Rubottom. West of Louis Phillips' home he built a house and a tavern. As innkeeper he became one of the best known men in the county. His place was called Rubottom's, where the stages changed horses, but when a postoffice was established it became "Spadra," named for Spadra Bluffs in Arkansas, Uncle Billy's home town.

One of the first of the incoming Americans to make a settlement within Pomona's present limits was Robert S. Arnett. In 1868 he bought seventy acres in the Palomares portion, the description in his deed beginning

"46 Spanish varas in a northerly direction
from a clump of sycamore trees all springing
from one root."

P. C. Tonner, the young Irishman who in later years was to win local fame through poetry, teaching and the real estate business, made his first visit to the valley in 1869.

Cyrus Burdick came in 1870, settling in the Ganesha Park area, planting orange trees and helping to turn a cattle ranch into a fruit orchard.

He was followed by Charles F. Loop and Alvin R. Meserve, who, in 1873, bought two thousand acres (lying between Pomona and Claremont). Under their direction the "Loop and Meserve Tract" bloomed with grapes, oranges, lemons and olives.

In 1873, Louis Phillips had given the Southern Pacific railroad a right of way through the Pomona area.

Now the whole San José Valley began to think in terms of "town."

A small group of southern California men, some of whose names are perpetuated in Pomona's streets, decided that the San José Ranch, with its good setting, its fertile acres and a railroad about to be built, was ripe for colonization and town building.

The articles of incorporation of The Los Angeles Immigration and Land Co-Operative Association announced as its purpose:

"To circulate information throughout this and other counties regarding southern California and to promote immigration hereto, to buy and sell real estate, to sell real estate on a commission, and to do any other business incidental to carrying on a real estate business."

The Association, organized in 1874, was capitalized at $250,000.00, divided into 2500 shares of $100.00 each.

The seven original directors were: J. E. McComas (Compton), J. T. Gordon (Azusa), Geo. C. Gibbs (San Gabriel Mission), T. A. Garey, Milton Thomas, H. J. Crow and R. M. Town (all of Los Angeles).

The president was Garey and the secretary L. M. Holt.

The first train from Los Angeles to Spadra ran on January 21, 1874, according to Southern Pacific records.

*1874
Railroad*

With its organization completed, the Association in April of 1875 obtained a contract of sale from Louis Phillips covering the valley plain upon which it was planned to bring settlers and start a town. This property lay south of the Southern Pacific Railroad Company's right of way. Under another contract the Association obtained the right of purchasing certain property north of the railroad in which Tonner, Burdick and Palomares were interested, as well as Louis Phillips.

A civil engineer, A. Higbie, was employed to survey and subdivide twenty-five hundred acres. He and his assistants went forth with transit and tape. Upon the land where sheep and cattle had been grazing since 1837 a town was outlined. The streets and blocks and lots that make up Pomona were marked and staked and before the end of July in 1875 a map was turned over to the Association.

The new town was bounded by Artesia Boulevard (now San Antonio Avenue) on the east, Phillips Boulevard on the south, Hamilton Boulevard on the west and by the old dividing line between the Vejar and Palomares properties on the north. This line was about two blocks north of Holt Avenue. Outside these town boundaries lay the forty-acre lots that were to draw the more ambitious of the fruit growers.

Before the birth of the town a name was chosen.

The promoters thought "Palomares" had a pleasant sound, but decided on a name contest, with a free lot as a prize.

Solomon Gates, a nurseryman, came forth with an

appropriate and winning suggestion: "Pomona, Goddess of Fruit."

Pomona it became—out of Roman mythology—and
on August 20, 1875, it was given public record by L. M.
Holt filing the approved map with the County Recorder at Los Angeles.

When a hotel had been built at the corner of Fifth
Street and Garey Avenue, when a grocery, a drug and
provision store, a dry goods shop, a meat market, a
blacksmith shop and a dozen dwellings had sprung into
being, when a few artesian wells had been sunk and a
reservoir constructed, Pomona was ready to declare
herself before the world. Posters throughout southern
California announced that the grand opening and public
auction sale of lots would be held on Washington's
Birthday, February 22, 1876. From Los Angeles, an
excursion was to be run.

On that Washington's Birthday most of Pomona
and the plain surrounding was carpeted with wild grass:
the alfilaria that had fattened the rancheros' cattle. There
were brilliant beds of poppies and cream cups in abun-
dance. There were freshly graded streets. Water was
flowing in open irrigation ditches. There were car-
riages and drivers to handle throngs of excursionists.
At the hotel free dinners were being prepared. Children
picked bouquets, bands played, salesmen orated, auc-
tioneers' hammers rose and fell, and about nineteen
thousand dollars' worth of land was sold.

Drought years, a disastrous fire and the exhaustion
of the promoters' money, however, almost ruined Po-

mona before she was two years old. By 1880 the
population was only 130.

1882
New
Life
The arrival of Dr. Cyrus T. Mills in 1882, his association with M. L. Wicks, and the organization in that
year of the Pomona Land and Water Company put new
life into the town that was named after the goddess
of fruits and gardens.

Mills and Wicks bought out the Louis Phillips', the
Palomares' and the subdividers' interests in Pomona and
adjacent land and then placed title in the new corporation. They obtained water rights, and with plenty of
water from mountains, ciénegas and artesian wells
Pomona grew and prospered.

1887
Incor-
poration
By 1887, the year of incorporation as a city, Pomona's people numbered 3500. There were schools,
banks, nurseries, newspapers, livery stables, feed-mills,
churches, lodges, brickyards, fruit canneries, confec-
tioneries and hotels. One of the latter was the Palomares, given a brilliant opening by Frank Miller of later
Mission Inn fame.

That was the year, too, of the beginning of the
Great Boom, about to rage through southern California,
due to leave much wreckage on the domain of Ricardo Vejar, Ygnacio Palomares and Louis Phillips, but
also to shape the foundations of modern Pomona.

Today
*Pomona draws her strength from the soil of "the
place called San José" into which, in 1837, Ricardo
Vejar and Ygnacio Palomares brought families, vaqueros
and herds of cattle and sheep. Today, as then, Pomona's*

land lies in the arms of oak-strewn hills, with mountains looming high on the north. Twenty-two thousand people are now assembled on this sheep and cattle ranch of Mexican days. They have made of their rich, ripe inheritance an orchard and a garden, and throughout the year they gather full crops from thirty thousand acres of orange, lemon and walnut trees, from abundant plantings of beans and tomatoes. They have raised fine horses and cattle. They have held annually a county fair devoted to agriculture, live-stock and the arts and crafts. They have developed schools and colleges of nation-wide distinction. They have made a city of broad, shaded streets, parks, good homes and active living.

Appendix

COMPLETE LIST OF THE RANCHOS
OF LOS ANGELES COUNTY

The following list of ranchos or land grants within, or partly within, the present boundaries of Los Angeles County includes only those that originated in concessions or grants of the Spanish and Mexican periods the titles to which were confirmed later by the United States Government. It does not include those abandoned prior to the American period, nor those the claims to which were rejected by the United States, nor town lots granted by pueblo authorities.

The name of the rancho or land grant, the acreage, and the person to whom a patent was issued are shown. In most instances the patentee is not the first owner. The small tracts, those less than one hundred acres in extent, are located at or near San Gabriel.

Rancho or Tract	Acreage	Patentee
AGUAJE DE LA CENTINELA	2219.26	Bruno Abila
AGUILAR TRACT (See Note at end of list)		
ALAMITOS (See LOS ALAMITOS)		
ALAMOS (See LOS ALAMOS Y AGUA CALIENTE)		
AZUSA DE DALTON	4431.47	Henry Dalton
AZUSA DE DUARTE	6595.62	Andrés Duarte
BALLONA (See LA BALLONA)		
BOCA DE SANTA MONICA	6656.93	Ysidro Reyes and Maria Roque Marquez

		ceased; and Rita, minor daughter and only legal heir of (the Indian) Francisco, deceased.
EL ESCORPION	1109.65	(Indians) Urbano, 2/12, Odon, 2/12, and Manuel, 3/12; and, also, Joaquin Romero, 5/12.
ENCINO (See EL ENCINO)		
ESCORPION (See EL ESCORPION)		
EX-MISSION DE SAN FERNANDO	116,858.46	Eulogio de Celis
FELIS (See LOS FELIS)		
HUERTA DE CUATI	128.26	Victoria Reid
ISLA DE SANTA CATALINA	45,825.43	José Maria Covarrubias
LA BALLONA	13,919.90	Augustin Machado
		Ygnacio Machado
		Felipe Talamantes
		Tomas Talamantes
LA BREA	4439.07	Antonio José Rocha
		José Jorge Rocha
		Josefa de la Merced Jordan
LA CANADA	5832.10	Jonathan Scott
		Benjamin Hayes
LA CIENEGA or PASO DE LA TIJERA (LA CIENEGA O PASO DE TIJERA)	4481.05	Tomas Sanchez
		Luisa Sanchez
		Juana Sanchez
		Josefa Sanchez
		Felipe Sanchez
		Victoria Higuera
LA HABRA	6698.57	Andrés Pico and Francesca Uribe de Ocampo, wife of Francisco Ocampo, deceased
LA LIEBRE	48,799.59	José Maria Flores

LA MERCED	2363.75	F. P. F. Temple
		Juan Matias Sanchez
LA PUENTE	48,790.55	John Rowland
		Julian Workman
LAS CIENEGAS	4439.05	Januario Abila and his three sisters Pedra Abila de Ramirez, Francesca Abila de Rimpau, and Luisa Abila de Garfias
LAS VIRGENES	8878.76	Maria Antonio Machado
LEDESMA TRACT	22.21	José Ledesma
LIEBRE (See LA LIEBRE)		
LOS ALAMITOS	17,789.79	Abel Stearns
LOS ALAMOS Y AGUA CALIENTE	26,626.23	Augustin Olvera
LOS ANGELES, PUEBLO DE	17,172.37	The Mayor and Common Council of the City of Los Angeles
LOS CERRITOS	27,054.36	Juan Temple
LOS COYOTES	48,806.17	Andrés Pico and Francesca Uribe de Ocampo, wife of Francisco Ocampo
LOS FELIS	6647.46	Maria Ygnacio Verdugo
LOS NOGALES	1003.67	Maria de Jesus Garcia
LOS PALOS VERDES	31,629.13	José Loreto Sepulveda
		Juan Sepulveda
MALIBU (See TOPANGA MALIBU SEQUIT)		
NOGALES (See LOS NOGALES)		
O PASO DE LA TIJERA (See LA CIENEGA)		
ORIZABA TRACT	179.60	Daniel Sexton
PALOS VERDES (See LOS PALOS VERDES)		
PASO DE BARTOLO (Guirado)	875.99	Bernardino Guirado
PASO DE BARTOLO (Pico)	8991.22	Pio Pico and Juan Perez

PASO DE LA TIJERA
  (See LA CIENEGA)

POTRERO CHICO   83.46   Antonio Valenzuela
                                 Juan Alvitre

POTRERO DE FELIPE
  LUGO   2042.81   George Morrillo
                                 Maria V. Romero

POTRERO GRANDE   4431.95   Juan Matias Sanchez

PROSPERO TRACT   23.68   Rafaela Valenzuela, widow,
                                 Juana Dominguez, wife of
                                   Vicente Duarte,
                                 Juana Dominguez, wife of
                                 Pio Silvas,
                                 Maria Ygnacia,
                                 Liberata,
                                 Jesus,
                                 Rosares, and
                                 Candelaria, heirs of the In-
                                 dian Prospero, deceased.

PROVIDENCIA   4064.33   David W. Alexander
                                 Francis Mellus

PUENTE (See LA PUENTE)

REDONDO (See
  SAUSAL REDONDO)

RINCON DE LA BREA   4452.59   Gil Ybara

RINCON DE LOS BUEYES 3127.09   Francisco Higuera
                                 Secundino Higuera

RODEO DE LAS AGUAS 4449.31   Maria Rita Valdez

SALES TRACT   19.43   Francisco Sales

SAN ANTONIO (Lugo) 29,513.35   Antonio Maria Lugo

SAN ANTONIO (Valdez)—
  (See RODEO DE LAS
  AGUAS)

SAN FERNANDO (See
  EX-MISSION DE SAN
  FERNANDO)

SAN FERNANDO MISSION
  (Church property)   170.20   Joseph S. Alemany,
                                 Bishop of Monterey

SAN FRANCISCO	48,611.88	Jacoba Felis
		Ygnacio del Valle
		Maria del Valle
		Magdalena del Valle
		José Antonio del Valle
		José Ygnacio del Valle
		Concepcion del Valle
SAN FRANCISQUITO	8893.62	Henry Dalton
SAN GABRIEL MISSION		
(Church property)	33.34	Joseph S. Alemany,
		Bishop of Monterey
SAN JOSE	22,340.41	Ygnacio Palomares
		Ricardo Vejar
		Henry Dalton
SAN JOSE ADDITION	4430.64	Henry Dalton
		Ygnacio Palomares
		Ricardo Vejar
SAN JOSE DE		
BUENOS AYRES	4438.69	Benjamin D. Wilson
		William T. B. Sanford
SAN PASQUAL	13,693.93	Manuel Garfias
SAN PASQUALITA	708.57	Benjamin D. Wilson (claim-
		ant in place of Juan Gal-
		lardo)
SAN PEDRO	43,119.13	Manuel Dominguez
		Concepcion Rocha
		Bernardino Rocha
		José Antonio Aguirra
		Maria Jesus Cota de
		Dominguez
		Madalina Dominguez
		Andrés Dominguez
		Feliciana Dominguez
		Esteban Dominguez
		Maria Dominguez
		Pedro Dominguez
		José Dominguez
		Maria, widow of Manuel
		Rocha
		Antonio Jacinto Rocha

SAN RAFAEL	36,403.32	Julio Verdugo
		Catalina Verdugo
SAN VICENTE Y SANTA MONICA	30,259.65	Ramona Sepulveda, widow of Francisco Sepulveda
SANTA ANITA	13,319.06	Henry Dalton
SANTA CATALINA (See ISLA DE SANTA CATALINA)		
SANTA GERTRUDES (Colima)	3696.23	Tomas Sanchez Colima
SANTA GERTRUDES (McFarland and Downey)	17,602.01	James P. McFarland
		John G. Downey
SANTA MONICA (See BOCA DE SANTA MONICA and SAN VICENTE Y SANTA MONICA)		
SAUSAL REDONDO	22,458.94	Antonio Ygnacio Abila
SEXTON TRACT (Also see ORIZABA TRACT)	48.18	Daniel Sexton
SIMEON TRACT	30.45	Simeon, an Indian
SIMI	113,009.21	José de la Guerra y Noriega
TAJAUTA	3559.86	Enrique Abila, executor of the last will and testament of Anastacio Abila, deceased
TEMESCAL	13,339.07	Ramon de la Cuesta
		Francisco Gonzales Camino
TOPANGA MALIBU SEQUIT	13,315.70	Matthew Keller
TUJUNGA	6660.71	David W. Alexander
		Francis Mellus and Augustin Olvera for themselves and the heirs of Francisco Lopez, deceased
VIRGENES (See LAS VIRGENES)		

VOCA DE SANTA
  MONICA (See BOCA
  DE SANTA MONICA)
WHITE TRACT   77.23   Michael White

(Note: The AGUILAR TRACT, on the list of the General Land
    Office, does not appear to be listed in the Los Angeles County
    Recorder's index to patents of Los Angeles County. This was
    a tract 500 varas by 250 varas in extent near San Gabriel, in Los
    Angeles County, the claimants to which were Lugardo Aguilar
    and Pascuala Garcia, his wife.)

COMPLETE LIST OF RANCHOS OF CALIFORNIA

The following list of the ranchos of California is that compiled by the General Land Office in 1928 under the title of "Private Land Grants". Like the Los Angeles County list preceding, it obviously includes only those that originated in concessions or grants of the Spanish and Mexican periods the titles to which were confirmed later by the United States Government.

Acalanes
Agua Caliente
   (in Sonoma County)
Agua Caliente
   (in Alameda County)
Aguaje de Centinela
Aguas Frias
Agua Hedionda
Aguajit
Agua Puerca y las Trancas
Aptos
Arroyo Chico
Arroyo de la Alameda
Arroyo de la Laguna
Arroyo de las Nueces y Bolbones
Arroyo del Rodeo
Arroyo Grande
Arroyo Seco
Arroyo Seco (Torre)
Asuncion
Azusa (Dalton)
Azusa (Duarte)
Atascadero
Ausaymas y San Felipe
Ballona
Blucher
Boca de la Playa
Boca de Santa Monica
Bodega
Boga

Bolsa de Chamisal
Bolsa de las Escorpinas
Bolsa del Pajaro
Bolsa del Potrero y Moro Cojo or
   La Sagrada Familia
Bolsa de San Cayetano
Bolsa de San Felipe
Bolsa Nuevo y Moro Cojo
Bosquejo
Buena Vista
   (in San Diego County)
Buena Vista
   (in Monterey County)
Buri Buri
Butano
Cabeza de Santa Rosa
Cahuenga
Calleguas
Camaritas, in San Francisco
Campo de los Franceses
Cañada de Capay
Cañada de Guadalupe y Rodeo
   Viejo
Cañada de Guadalupe la Visita-
   cion y Rodeo Viejo
Cañada de Herrera
Cañada de Jonive
Cañada de la Carpinteria
Cañada de la Segunda
Cañada del Corral

Cañada del Corte de Madera
Cañada del Hambre y las Bolsas
Cañada de los Alisos
Cañada de los Capitancillos
Cañada de los Coches
Cañada de los Nogales
Cañada de los Osos y Pecho y Islay
Cañada de los Piños or College Rancho (Church property)
Cañada de los Vaqueros
Cañada del Rincon en el Rio San Lorenzo de Santa Cruz
Cañada de Pala
Cañada de Pogolimi
Cañada de Raymundo
Cañada de Salsipuedes
Cañada de San Felipe y Las Animas
Cañada de San Miguelito
Cañada de San Vicente y Mesa del Padre Barona
Cañada de Verde y Arroyo de la Purisima
Cañada Larga o' Verde
Collayomi
Colus
Cañon de Santa Ana
Capay
Carne Humana
Caslamayomi
Casmalia
Castac
Catacula
Caymus
Chimiles
Cholame
Chualar
Ciénega del Gabilan
Ciénega de los Paicines
Ciénega o Paso de la Tijera
Corral de Piedra

Corral de Quati
Corral de Tierra (McCobb)
Corral de Tierra (Palomares)
Corral de Tierra (Vasquez)
Corte Madera de Novata
Corte de Madera del Presidio
Cosumnes
Cotate
Cucamonga
Cuca or El Potrero
Cuyama (Heirs of Cesario Lataillade)
Cuyama (M. A. de la G. y Lataillade)
Cuyamaca
Del Paso
El Alisal (Bernal)
El Alisal (Hartnell)
El Cajon
El Chamisal
El Chorro
El Conejo
El Corte de Madera
El Encino
El Escorpion
El Sobrante
El Pescadero (Grimes)
El Pescadero (Jacks)
El Pescadero (Pico and Naglee)
El Piojo
El Potrero de San Carlos
El Potrero de Santa Clara
El Primer Cañon or Rio de Los Berrendos
El Rincon
El Rincon (Arellanes)
El Sur
El Tejon
El Toro
El Tucho
Encinal y Buena Esperanza
Entre Napa

Entre Napa or Rincon de los
  Carneros
Esquon
Estero Americano
Ex-Mission de San Fernando
Ex-Mission San Buenaventura,
  Lands of
Ex-Mission San Juan Capistrano,
  Three tracts at, (Church
  property)
Ex-Mission San Diego, Three
  tracts at, (Church property)
Ex-Mission San Luis Rey, Four
  tracts at, (Church property)
Ex-Mission Soledad
Feliz
Fernandez
German
Guadalasca
Guadalupe
Guadalupe y Llanitos de los
  Correos
Guajome
Guejito
Guenoc
Guesisosi
Honcut
Huasna
Huerhuero
Huerta de Cuati
Huerta de Romualdo or El
  Chorro
Huichica
Jacinto
Jamacho
Jamul
Jesus Maria
Jimeno
Johnson Rancho
Juristac
Jurupa (Stearns)
Jurupa (Roubideau)

La Barranca Colorado
La Boca de la Cañada del Pinole
La Bolsa Chica
La Brea
Lac
La Cañada
La Carbonera
La Goleta
Laguna (Church Property)
Laguna de la Merced
Laguna de las Calabasas
Laguna de los Palos Colorados
Laguna de San Antonio
Laguna de Tache
Laguna Seca
La Habra
La Jota
La Laguna (Gutierrez)
La Laguna Seca
La Laguna (Stearns)
La Liebre
La Merced
La Mission Vieja de la Purisima
La Nacion
La Natividad
La Polka
La Puente
La Purisima Concepcion
Larkin's Children's Rancho
Las Animas
Las Baulines
Las Bolsas
Las Ciénegas
Las Ciénegitas
Las Cruces
Las Flores
Las Juntas
Las Mariposas
Las Pocas
Las Positas
Las Positas y la Calera
Las Putas

Las Salinas
La Sierra (Sepulveda)
La Sierra (Yorba)
Las Uvas
Las Virgenes
La Zaca
Llano de Buena Vista
Llano de Santa Rosa
Llano del Tequisquita
Llano Seco
Locoallomi
Lomas de la Purificacion
Lomas de Santiago
Lomerias Muertas
Lompoc
Los Alamitos
Los Alamos
Los Alamos y Agua Caliente
Los Angeles, City Lands of,
Las Aromitas y Agua Caliente
Los Capitancillos
Los Carneros (Littlejohn)
Los Carneros (McDougal)
Los Cerritos
Los Coches
    (in Santa Clara County)
Los Coches
    (in Monterey County)
Los Corralitos
Los Coyotes
Los Dos Pueblos
Los Encenitos
Los Felis
Los Gatos or Santa Rita
Los Guilicos
Los Huecos
Los Laurelles (Beronda)
Los Laurelles (Ransom)
Los Medanos
Los Meganos
Los Nogales
Los Ojitos

Los Palos Verdes
Los Penasquitos
Los Prietos y Najalayegua
Los Putos
Los Tularcitos (Gomez)
Los Ulpinos
Los Vallecitos de San Marcos
Los Vergeles
Mallacomes or Moristul
Mallacomes or Moristul y Plan
    de Agua Caliente
Meadows Tract
Mesa de Ojo de Agua
Milpitas
Milpitas (Alviso)
Miramontes
Mission Carmelo (Church
    property)
Mission Dolores, Fifty Vara Lot
    in, (De Haro)
Mission Dolores, Suerte in,
Mission Dolores, Tract of Land
    in, (Bernal)
Mission Dolores, Two Lots in,
    (De Haro)
Mission Dolores, Two Tracts at,
    (Church property)
Mission la Purisima
Mission la Purisima, Land of,
    (Church property)
Mission of San Gabriel (Church
    property)
Mission of Santa Ynez, Lands of,
Mission San Antonio (Church
    property)
Mission San Diego
Mission San Fernando, Eight
    Tracts at, (Church
    property)
Mission San José, Three Tracts
    at, (Church property)

Mission San Juan Bautista, Tracts at, (Church property)
Mission San Juan Capistrano, Five Tracts at, (Church property)
Mission San Miguel (Church property)
Mission San Rafael, Mission Lands, (Church property)
Mission Santa Barbara, Lands of, (Church property)
Mission San Buenaventura, Lands of, (Church property)
Mission Soledad, Two Tracts at, (Church property)
Mission Viejo or La Paz
Molinos
Monserate
Monte del Diablo
Monterey, City Lands of,
Monterey County, Tract of Land in, (Castro)
Monterey County, Tract of Land in, (Cocks)
Moro y Cayucos
Muniz
Muscupiabe
Nacional
Napa
New Helvetia, Two tracts,
Nicasio
Niguel
Nipoma
Noche Buena
Nojoqui
Novato
Nuestra Señora del Refugio
Ojai
Ojo de Agua de Figueroa, in San Francisco,
Ojo de Agua de la Coche
Olompali
Omochumnes

One Suerte
Orestimba
Otay (Dominguez)
Otay (Estudillo)
Pala
Panoche de San Juan y los Carrisalitos
Paraje de Sanchez
Paso de Bartolo (Guirado)
Paso de Bartolo (Pico)
Paso de Bartolo (Sepulveda)
Paso de Robles
Pastoria de las Borregas (Castro part and Murphy part)
Pauba
Pauma
Petaluma
Piedra Blanca
Pinole
Pismo
Pleyto
Posa de los Ositos
Posolmi
Potrero Chico
Potrero de Felipe Lugo
Potrero de los Cerritos
Potrero de San Luis Obispo
Potrero Grande
Potreros of San Juan Capistrano
Potrero y Rincon de San Pedro de Reglado
Prospero Tract
Providencia
Pueblo of San Francisco
Pueblo Lands of San José
Pueblo Lands of Santa Barbara
Pueblo Lands of Sonoma
Pueblo Lot No. 6
Pulgas
Punta del Ano Nuevo
Punta de la Concepcion
Punta de la Laguna

Punta de los Reyes
Punta de los Reyes (Sobrante)
Punta de Pinos
Punta de Quentin
Quito
Rancheria del Rio Estanislao
Ranchita de Santa Fe
Rancho de Farwell
Rancho del Puerto
Real de las Aguilas
Refugio
Rinconada del Arroyo de San
 Francisquito
Rinconada de los Gatos
Rincon de la Brea
Rincon de la Puente del Monte
Rincon de las Salinas
Rincon de las Salinas y Potrero
 Viejo
Rincon del Diablo
Rincon de los Bueyes
Rincon de los Esteros (Alviso)
Rincon de los Esteros
 (Berreyesa)
Rincon de los Esteros (White)
Rincon de Musalacon
Rincon de San Francisquito
Rincon de Sanjon
Rio de los Americanos
Rio de los Molinos
Rio de los Putos
Rio de Santa Clara
Rio Jesus Maria
Roblar de la Miseria
Salsipuedes
Sausal Redondo
San Andrés
San Antonio (A. M. Peralta)
San Antonio (Lugo)
San Antonio (Mesa)
San Antonio or Pescadero

San Antonio or Rodeo de las
 Aguas
San Antonio (V. & D. Peralta)
San Antonio (Y. Peralta)
San Augustin
San Benito
San Bernabe
San Bernardino
San Bernardo (Cane)
San Bernardo (Snook)
San Bernardo (Soberanes)
San Buenaventura
San Carlos de Jonata
Sancito
San Diegito
San Diego, Island or Peninsula of,
San Diego, Pueblo Lands of,
Sanel
San Emidio
San Francisco
San Francisco de las Llagas
San Francisco Solano, in Sonoma,
 Mission Lands (Church
 property)
San Francisco, Two Lots in,
 (Leese)
San Francisquito
San Francisquito (Dalton)
San Francisquito (Rodriguez)
San Gabriel, Tract of Land near,
 (Aguilar)
San Gabriel, Tract of Land near,
 (Courtney)
San Gabriel, Tract of Land near,
 (Domingo)
San Gabriel, Tract of Land near,
 (Ledesma)
San Gabriel, Tract of Land near,
 (Sales)
San Gabriel, Tract of Land near,
 (Sexton)

San Gabriel, Tract of Land near,
(Simeon)
San Gabriel, Tract of Land near,
(White)
San Geronimo
(in Marin County)
San Geronimo
(in San Luis Obispo County)
San Gregorio (Castro)
San Gregorio (Rodriguez)
San Jacinto and San Gorgonio,
Tract between,
San Jacinto Nuevo y Potrero
San Jacinto Viejo
San Joaquin
(in Orange County)
San Joaquin
(in San Benito County)
Sanjon de los Moquelumnes
Sanjon de Santa Rita
San José, Addition to,
San José, (Dalton et al)
San José de Buenos Ayres
San José del Valle
San José (Pacheco)
San José y sur Chiquito
San Juan
San Juan Bautista
San Juan Bautista, Tract of Land
near,
San Juan Bautista, Tract of Land
near, (Breen)
San Juan Cajon de Santa Ana
San Julian
San Justo
San Leandro
San Lorenzo (Castro)
San Lorenzo (Randall)
San Lorenzo (Sanchez)
San Lorenzo (Soberanes)
San Lorenzo (Soto)
San Lucas

San Luis Gonzaga
San Luisito
San Luis Obispo, Mission Lands
of, (Church property)
San Mateo
San Miguel (West)
San Miguel (Noe)
San Miguel (Olivas and
Lorenzana)
San Marcos
San Miguelito
(in San Luis Obispo County)
San Miguelito
(in Monterey County)
San Pablo
San Pasqual (Garfias)
San Pasqual (Wilson)
San Pedro (Dominguez)
San Pedro (Sanchez)
San Pedro, Santa Margarita y las
Gallinas
San Rafael
San Ramon (Amador)
San Ramon (Carpentier)
San Ramon (Norris)
San Simeon
Santa Ana
Santa Ana del Chino
Santa Ana del Chino, Addition
to,
Santa Ana y Quien Sabe
Santa Anita
Santa Catalina Island
Santa Clara del Norte
Santa Clara, Tract of Land near,
(Enright)
Santa Clara County, Two Tracts
in, (Bennett)
Santa Clara, Two Mission Tracts
in, (Church property)
Santa Cruz, Island of,

Santa Cruz, Mission Lands of,
   (Church property)
Santa Gertrudes (Colima)
Santa Gertrudes (McFarland
   and Downey)
Santa Manuela
Santa Margarita
Santa Margarita y Las Flores
Santa Paula y Saticoy
Santa Rita
Santa Rita (Malo)
Santa Rosa (Cota)
Santa Rosa (Estrada)
Santa Rosa, Island of,
Santa Rosa (Morino)
Santa Teresa
Santa Ysabel
   (in San Diego County)
Santa Ysabel
   (in San Luis Obispo County)
Santiago de Santa Ana
San Vicente (Berreyesa)
San Vicente (Escarrilla)
San Vicente (Munrass)
San Vicente y Santa Monica
San Ysidro (Gilroy)
San Ysidro (Ortega)
Saucelito
Saucos
Sausal
Sespe
Shoquel
Shoquel Augmentation
Simi
Sisquoc
Sobrante de San Jacinto
Soledad, Ex-Mission,
Solis
Sonoma City, Lot in,
Sotoyome

Soulajule
Stanislaus River, Eight Square
   Leagues on,
Suey
Suisun
Tajauta
Temecula
Temescal
Tepusquet
Tequepis
Tinaquaic
Todos Santos y San Antonio
Tolenas
Tomales y Baulines (Garcia)
Tomales y Baulines (Phelps)
Topanga Malibu Sequit
Trabuco
Tract of Land 1000 varas square
   (Sexton)
Tres Ojos de Agua
Tujunga
Tularcitos (Higuera)
Tulucay
Two Suertes
Tzabaco
Ulistac
Valle de Pamo or Santa Maria
Valle de San José (Portilla)
Valle de San José (Sunol &
   Bernal)
Valley of Temecula, Lands in
   the,
Valle de San Felipe
Vega del Rio del Pajaro
Yajome
Yerba Buena
Yokaya
Yosemite and Big Tree Grants
Zanjones
Zayanta

INDEX

235

LOS ANGELES COUNTY
Showing
RANCHOS and CITIES

Alhambra	1	Los Nietos	71	
Altadena	2	Lynwood	37	
Arcadia	3	Manhattan Beach	38	
Artesia	4	Maywood	39	
Avalon	5	Monrovia	40	
Azusa	6	Montebello	41	
Baldwin Park	7	Monterey Park	42	
Bel-Air	70	North Hollywood	43	
Bell	8	Northridge	44	
Beverly Hills	9	Norwalk	45	
Burbank	10	Pacoima	46	
Calabasas	11	Palms	72	
Canoga Park	12	Pasadena	47	
Chatsworth Park	13	Pomona	48	
Claremont	14	Puente	49	
Clearwater	15	Reseda	50	
Compton	16	Redondo Beach	51	
Covina	17	Rivera	73	
Culver City	18	Roscoe	52	
Downey	19	San Dimas	53	
El Monte	20	San Fernando	54	
El Segundo	21	San Gabriel	55	
Encino	22	San Marino	56	
Gardena	23	San Pedro	57	
Girard	24	Santa Monica	58	
Glendale	25	Sierra Madre	59	
Glendora	26	South Gate	60	
Hawthorne	27	South Pasadena	61	
Hermosa Beach	28	Studio City	62	
Hollywood	29	Sunland	63	
Huntington Park	30	Tarzana	64	
Inglewood	31	Torrance	65	
La Cañada	32	Van Nuys	66	
La Crescenta	33	Venice	74	
La Verne	34	Westwood	67	
Long Beach	35	Whittier	68	
Los Angeles	36	Wilmington	69	

COUNTY

El

El Conejo

Topanga Ma